T0248069

Bend the Knee or Seize the Throne

EXPLORING EFFECTIVE LEADERSHIP PRACTICES THROUGH POPULAR CULTURE

Series Editor: Michael Urick

The aim of this series is to examine modern and innovative business theories and methods via relatable popular cultural themes. The books will provide academically rigorous and credible applications and solutions to practitioners and upper-level business students, in a format designed to be highly engaging and effective.

Titles in Exploring Effective Leadership Practices Through Popular Culture

A Manager's Guide to Using the Force: Leadership Lessons from a Galaxy Far Far Away
Michael Urick

Leadership in Middle Earth: Theories and Applications for Organizations
Michael Urick

Leadership Insights for Wizards and Witches
Aditya Simha

Leaders Assemble! Leadership in the MCU
Gordon B. Schmidt and *Sy Islam*

Bend the Knee or Seize the Throne: Leadership Lessons from the Seven Kingdoms
Nathan Tong and *Michael Urick*

Forthcoming

Against All Odds: Leadership and the Handmaid's Tale
Cristina de Mello-e-Souza Wildermuth

Cross-cultural Leadership in the Four Nations: Lessons From Avatar The Last Airbender
Sy Islam and *Gordon B. Schmidt*

Slaying the Vampires, Werewolves and Demons of Ineffective Leadership
Aditya Simha

Bend the Knee or Seize the Throne: Leadership Lessons from the Seven Kingdoms

BY

NATHAN TONG
ESSCA School of Management, France

AND

MICHAEL J. URICK
Alex G. McKenna School of Business, Economics, and Government, Saint Vincent College, USA

United Kingdom – North America – Japan – India – Malaysia – China

Emerald Publishing Limited
Howard House, Wagon Lane, Bingley BD16 1WA, UK

First edition 2023

Reprints and permissions service
Contact: permissions@emeraldinsight.com

British Library Cataloguing in Publication Data
A catalogue record for this book is available from the British Library

ISBN: 978-1-80262-650-6 (Print)
ISBN: 978-1-80262-647-6 (Online)
ISBN: 978-1-80262-649-0 (Epub)

ISOQAR certified
Management System,
awarded to Emerald
for adherence to
Environmental
standard
ISO 14001:2004.

Certificate Number 1985
ISO 14001

INVESTOR IN PEOPLE

This book is dedicated to my family and loved ones who have supported me through thick and thin. I wouldn't be where I am in life today without you. Thank you for being there for me and for being my cheerleaders behind the scenes. And to Spot and Aibi in particular; thank you for watching *Game of Thrones* with me, even though you had no idea what was going on.—NT

I dedicate this book to all my friends who shared in (over)analyzing *Game of Thrones* every time we saw a new episode, especially Jim, Dave, and Nick. Thanks for sharing your time, energy, and happiness with me, not only in watching and/or discussing the show, but in all aspects of our friendship.—MJU

Contents

About the Authors

Dr Nathan Tong, PhD, MBA, is an Associate Professor of Management at ESSCA School of Management at the school's Lyon campus in France. He received his PhD in Business Administration (Management/Organizational Behavior focus) from the Lindner College of Business at the University of Cincinnati. His MBA is from the Liautaud Graduate School of Business at the University of Illinois at Chicago and his bachelor's degree in Psychology is from John Muir College at the University of California San Diego.

His research interests include organizational justice and fairness, non-traditional work arrangements, and workplace interactions and relationships. His work has appeared in *Academy of Management Review* as well as *The Oxford Handbook of Justice in the Workplace*. He regularly presents his work at the annual Academy of Management conference, as well as other regional and international academic conferences. Currently, he teaches courses in Organizational Behavior and Leadership. He has also taught courses on Human Resources, Organizational Strategy, and various introduction to business courses, and led workshops on leadership and teams.

Dr Michael J. Urick, PhD, MBA, MS, SSGB, is Dean of the Alex G. McKenna School of Business, Economics, and Government at Saint Vincent College in Latrobe, PA as well as a Professor of Management and Operational Excellence.

He received his PhD in Management (Organizational Behavior focus) from the University of Cincinnati. His MBA (focused in Human Resources Management) and MS (in Leadership and Business Ethics) are both from Duquesne University in Pittsburgh, and his Bachelor's degree in Accounting with Management and English minors is from Saint Vincent College. Dr. Urick has taught undergraduate and graduate courses related to organizational behavior, human resources, communication, conflict, organizational culture, operations, and research methods.

The Master of Science in Management: Operational Excellence program at Saint Vincent, which he directed for nearly 10 years prior to his role as Dean, focuses on providing aspiring leaders with cutting-edge management techniques to effectively problem solve, minimize waste, and continuously improve their organizations. Under his directorship, the program was consistently ranked as a "Top 50 Best Value Master's in Management" program by Value Colleges and as a "Top Online Non-MBA Business Graduate Degree" by US News and World Report.

He is Six Sigma Green Belt Certified, Diversity Management Certified, a Certified Conflict Manager, Project Management Essentials Certified, and MBTI Certified, and is also certified through the Society for Human Resource Management as well as the True Lean program at the University of Kentucky. He is the recipient of an "Excellence in Teaching" Award from the Lindner College of Business at the University of Cincinnati, the "Quentin Schaut Faculty Award" from Saint Vincent College, and a "Teaching Excellence" Award from the Accreditation Council for Business Schools and Programs among other pedagogical honors. Internationally, he was also recognized by the Institute for Supply Management as a "Person of the Year" in the learning and education category.

Urick is an Associate Editor of the *Journal of Leadership and Management* based in Poland, the North American Associate Editor of the *Measuring Business Excellence* journal, and is on the Editorial Board of *Management Teaching Review*. He is also the Editor for the *Exploring Effective Leadership Practices Through Popular Culture* book series from Emerald Publishing.

His research interests include leadership, conflict, and identity in the workplace. Much of his work focuses on issues related to intergenerational phenomena within organizations. He also often examines how popular culture can be used to advance organizational behavior theory. In addition to authoring or co-authoring over 50 publications including multiple books and peer-reviewed articles, he has regularly presented at academic and practitioner international meetings such as the Academy of Management, Society for Industrial and Organizational Psychology, and Institute for Supply Management conferences. He is a regular speaker on age-related issues in the workplace throughout the United States and internationally (having presented on four continents) and served as a consultant on issues related to workplace interactions, organizational culture, and ethics for various organizations. He has served as a reviewer for a variety of academic publications including the *Journal of Intergenerational Relationships, Journal of Social Psychology, Journal of Organizational Behavior*, and *Journal of Family Issues* as well as the Organizational Behavior and Human Resources divisions of the Academy of Management Annual Meeting in addition to other conferences.

Professionally, he has served on the Boards of ISM-Pittsburgh (in various roles including President) and the Westmoreland Arts and Heritage Festival (a top-rated community event). He has also served on the Westmoreland Human Resources Association (a regional SHRM chapter) Board in various positions including Vice President. Prior to academia, Urick worked in a variety of roles related to auditing, utilities, environmental issues, and training and development. Through these experiences, Dr. Urick became fascinated with interactions in the workplace and how they might be improved which has influenced his academic career.

For fun, he enjoys music and, since 1998, has been a semi-professional jazz musician and toured through over a dozen US states while releasing multiple recordings with various ensembles.

Acknowledgments

Thank-yous

NT

My entire family, Yung, Rebecca, Ming-Jinn, Catherine, Tran, Rita, and the kids, who have all supported me while I've chased all my ambitions and dreams.

Dr. Mike Urick, my eternal gratitude for inviting me to be part of this phenomenal series and supporting me during the process.

All my friends who have listened to me talk about this book incessantly; it's finally here.

MJU

My family especially Janet, Lucy, Mickie, and Rick who were always supportive of my writing.

My colleagues, especially Dr John Delaney and the Faculty of the McKenna School at Saint Vincent, for being receptive to unique areas of leadership scholarship including those that examine pseudo-medieval fantasy fiction.

Dr Brigitte Biehl for her insights into leadership in *Game of Thrones*.

Both

We want to thank the team at Emerald Publishing, especially Fiona Allison, Dr Daniel Ridge, and Lydia Cutmore, for continuing to provide an outlet for this series of books that make academic theories and concepts accessible, relatable, and, most of all, fun for people to understand. Without these types of books, learning about leadership and management would largely remain in the classroom and from first-hand experience and mistakes. This series provides people the opportunity to learn about leadership through their favorite films, television shows, and other pop culture properties in a way we hope is entertaining and exciting.

We certainly cannot forget to thank George R. R. Martin, the entire team at HBO, and the extremely talented cast, crew, and countless other individuals who came together to create the magic that was, and still is, the *Game of Thrones* television series. Your imagination, hard work, and dedication created an amazing fantasy world for millions of people to escape into every week. We gasped, we cried, and we cheered for eight seasons, all thanks to your creativity, commitment, and passion to bring the world of Westeros to life. Thank you for sharing your talents with us.

Chapter 1

Introduction: Bend the Knee or Seize the Throne

Game of Thrones is one of the most-loved television shows in history and remains one of the most-awarded television shows ever. During its eight-season run from 2011 to 2019, it garnered a total of 160 Emmy nominations and 59 Emmy awards (emmys.com), more than any show in the history of television (except for *Saturday Night Live*, which has 338 Emmy awards, but has also been on the air continuously since 1975). In addition to these accolades, it remains one of the most-watched shows not only on HBO where it originally aired, but also in terms of television history. In 2019, over 30% of Americans said they were at least a casual fan of the show (statista.com). According to *The Hollywood Reporter*, the series has been seen by at least 44.2 million viewers (hollywoodreporter.com). This viewership is no small feat when you consider that the show's original run was primarily only available via HBO and not through on-demand streaming or free, publicly broadcast television channels.

Additionally, according to a 2017 survey conducted by *Rotten Tomatoes*, the popular movie and television ratings website, *Game of Thrones* came in at number 1 on its list of the 40 best shows of the last 20 years (rottentomatoes.com). *Rotten Tomatoes* said that the show "took [the] top spot with 11 percent of the vote, while second place [*Breaking Bad*] got 7 percent" (rottentomatoes.com). As another testament to the show's popularity and acclaim, it is also ranked as the number 1 television show of all time by IMDb (imdb.com), another popular movie and television ratings website, as of 2022. As these figures and awards indicate, *Game of Thrones* was, and still is, one of the most-watched and beloved shows in television history, admired by viewers and critics alike.

If you have picked up this book, then you are likely one of the millions of fans of *Game of Thrones*. You are also probably curious about what can be learned about management and leadership through the series and its cast of characters. *Game of Thrones* offers a plethora of examples of what can be achieved when leaders and managers act and lead people appropriately. It also provides numerous examples of how leaders and managers should *not* behave, along with a host of examples of negative consequences associated with poor leadership

Bend the Knee or Seize the Throne: Leadership Lessons from the Seven Kingdoms, 1–5
Copyright © 2023 by Nathan Tong and Michael J. Urick
Published under exclusive licence by Emerald Publishing Limited
doi:10.1108/978-1-80262-647-620231001

and inadequate management. In many situations, we, as leaders and managers, should "bend the knee" to our subordinates by uplifting them, prioritizing their needs over ours, and giving them control of decisions and resources in order for everyone to be able to achieve or accomplish bigger primary goals or objectives. Other times, it's necessary for us to "seize the throne" as organizational managers and leaders by taking the reins and controlling our employees' actions, making decisions for them, and allocating resources to them. But how do leaders know when to bend the knee versus when to seize the throne? In this book, we will explore different aspects of management and leadership and discuss why sometimes bending the knee is the optimal thing to do while other times, seizing the throne is the only option.

For those casual fans of the series who might not be as familiar with the show and its storyline, please be warned that this book contains spoilers. The plot of *Game of Thrones* centers around several groups of characters from the Seven Kingdoms of Westeros who are all fighting to reign from the Iron Throne after the death of King Robert Baratheon. Among them are Cersei Lannister, Daenerys Targaryen, and Stannis Baratheon, along with numerous others. The ruler of the Seven Kingdoms sits on the Iron Throne, a throne that was, according to Viserys Targaryen, one of the characters in the show, made of the swords of a thousand vanquished enemies, welded together by a fire from the breath of the greatest dragon. Each character vying to sit on the Iron Throne has seemingly compelling arguments as to why they are the rightful ruler of the Seven Kingdoms after King Robert's death. The cast of characters in the series also includes people who do not want to sit on the Iron Throne themselves but are motivated to take actions on behalf of someone else because they believe in the legitimacy of the claims of that person whom they are helping to ascend to the seat. Without these others, the would-be queens and kings would not necessarily be considered leaders because a leader without followers is just a party of one.

In this book, we will examine numerous characteristics and facets of management and leadership and explore how they are demonstrated and exhibited by various characters in *Game of Thrones*. However, it would be appropriate to first lay some groundwork to explain how leadership is different from management, define what leadership is, and to explore what effective leadership typically entails. First, what is the difference between leadership and management? Often, people refer to "leadership" when they say "management," as these two words are frequently used interchangeably. Certainly, exercising management involves exhibiting many characteristics associated with leadership. However, leading is different from managing. The role of a manager, or "managing," commonly entails executing plans (often created by others higher up in the organizational hierarchy), controlling resources (deciding who gets what and how much), and keeping track of people to ensure their actions are appropriate to achieve collective and/or organizational goals. In contrast, leadership includes a set of different actions such as motivating others (as opposed to simply controlling or tracking them), building trust between and among followers/employees through clear communication and ethical behaviors (instead of simply executing plans without considering people's strengths, weaknesses, personal goals, etc.), and helping others make sense of their environment.

You might be wondering what separates "regular" leadership from effective leadership? If leadership is about motivating others to achieve a common goal, then effective leadership can be thought of as getting others to motivate themselves to reach that goal. It also often entails showing them how they can achieve personal goals while simultaneously working toward the collective goal. Effective leadership essentially takes "regular" leadership and turns up the dial up a notch. Effective leaders work to build, and then work continuously to maintain, their followers' trust, as well as the trust between their followers. It's not enough for them to assume that any trust they build with and among others will sustain itself over time; they know it must be tended to in order to be maintained. Effective leadership also puts followers and their needs front and center. Leadership can get followers on board and have everyone moving in the same direction, but effective leadership considers what those followers need in order for them to achieve their individual maximum potential while optimizing each person's contribution to accomplishing the group's collective goals.

In *Game of Thrones*, Tyrion Lannister, one of the primary characters, once said that any man who needs to say out loud that he is the king, is no king. The same sentiment generally goes for leadership. Leaders should not need to say, "I am the leader" for others to recognize them as the leader. As we will see in this book, leaders are identified through their words and their actions. It is what they say and how they say it, in addition to what they do and how they do it, that differentiates leaders from followers, separates leaders from managers, and distinguishes good leaders from great leaders. The following paragraphs provide an overview of each chapter, and each one identifies a specific characteristic or aspect of leadership explored in that chapter.

In Chapter 2, we will explore different leadership styles and behaviors. We will provide labels and names to identify different styles of leadership, as well as discuss the various characteristics and behaviors each style of leadership entails. We will examine different characters in *Game of Thrones* and explain how they embody different leadership styles. We will also discuss the fact that leadership depends on followers. We will explain why there is no such thing as "one size fits all" leadership and examine why the best type of leadership in any given situation will depend on a number of factors, including the followers and their needs.

Chapter 3 examines power and influence. You have likely experienced power before, especially if you have ever been a manager or a leader, but it's even more likely that you have felt powerless at some point in your life. But have you ever given any thought to where power comes from? Why do some people have power while others do not? How can you gain power? How can you give away power, and why would anyone, let alone a leader, want to do so? This chapter will explore the different bases of power and how power can be used effectively to influence others.

Chapter 4 looks at leader emergence and sustainability. People often debate about whether leaders are made or born, contending that leaders are either born with certain unmalleable characteristics that make them leaders or that they are leaders as a result of their environment and experiences. This chapter takes a look at a variety of arguments along with what research has discovered about factors that can predict leader emergence, and factors that can lead to long-term sustainability in leadership positions.

Communication is the focus of Chapter 5. In our organizations, and indeed in our daily lives, we all need to communicate with others. Whether the communication is about a specific task that needs to be completed or about our feelings, opinions, and perceptions, communication is how information is transmitted from one party to another. No matter whether in verbal, written, or any other form, even the clearest of communications can fail when it is traveling from the sender to the receiver(s). In Chapter 5, we will break down what communication is, explore its different parts, explain why it's important in management and leadership, and investigate why and what might happen when communication goes wrong.

Chapter 6 brings ethics to the forefront. As a society, we are increasingly aware of the world around us, and to know better is to do better. As a result, we increasingly expect our leaders and organizations to behave ethically and make ethical decisions. But what is it exactly that we're judging when we evaluate other people (e.g., our managers and leaders) based on ethics? Against what standard(s) are we basing our evaluations? This chapter will explore ethics and why ethics matter to employees and their managers and leaders in organizations.

Because motivating others is one of the hallmarks of leadership, we will discuss motivation in Chapter 7. We know for ourselves what motivation feels like, but as a leader, how can you impart that sensation of drive and determination to others? This chapter will explain where motivation can stem from, what the determinants of motivation are, and how you can develop motivation in others so that they feel just as ambitious and excited as you do to work toward a collective goal.

Chapter 8 is about trust, because trust is imperative if one wants to be a good leader. No matter where you are in an organization, achieving organizational goals will ultimately require you to put your trust in others. Supervisors need to trust that their employees will perform their work duties to the best of their abilities, and employees need to trust that their supervisors have their best interests, along with the best interests of the organization, in mind as they make decisions and execute plans. This chapter explores the bases of trust and why trust matters, along with outcomes of placing (or misplacing) our trust in others.

We examine justice in Chapter 9. When people perceive they are treated fairly, they feel like they're valued, and people who feel valued in organizations tend to go the extra mile in their efforts because they want to give back to the person, group, and/or organization that values them. As inconceivable as it might seem, people still get treated unfairly at work. Chapter 9 explores why fair treatment matters, how justice perceptions are assessed (i.e., what perceptions of justice are based on), and the resulting outcomes associated with both fair and unfair treatment.

One of the important tasks managers and leaders must engage in is negotiation, so we explore this topic in Chapter 10. Although many people think of negotiation as an argument or a battle over limited resources, that is not at all what negotiation is about, nor is that how negotiations should be viewed.

Negotiations are opportunities to create situations in which parties can collaborate to create positive and mutually beneficial outcomes for everyone involved, rather than "fights" or battles where one party is trying to take advantage of another. This chapter will discuss why and how to approach negotiations so that the parties involved in the negotiation all walk away with something of more value than what they walked in with.

Finally, in Chapter 11, the importance of understanding and appreciating different national cultures is examined. With business becoming more and more interconnected around the world, it means organizations and managers need to do more than simply recognizing that cultural differences exist; they must also be sensitive to differences in culture and behave accordingly. Whether an organization wants to expand internationally, build new international partnerships, trade globally to sell products or source the best materials, or hire the best talent from around the world, it is imperative to be knowledgeable about and adaptive to other cultures. Organizational managers and leaders must not only acknowledge that cultural differences exist, but they must also practice cultural sensitivity to ensure that their words and actions (or those of their employees) do not come across as rude, condescending, inconsiderate, or offensive to business partners, job candidates, and other organizational prospects.

Now, before winter arrives and the White Walkers attempt to take control of everything, strap on your armor, ready your house banner, and let's set off for Westeros to learn what the queens, kings, knights, commoners, and even bastards of the Seven Kingdoms can teach us about managing and leadership.

Chapter 2

Leadership Styles and Behaviors

Throughout *Game of Thrones*, many of the primary characters in the series are fighting to sit on the Iron Throne to rule Westeros. Having a large cast of characters in the series affords us the opportunity to see a wide variety of leadership styles and their effectiveness (or ineffectiveness) in action. For example, the way Daenerys Targaryen demonstrates leadership with the Army of the Unsullied is markedly different from the way Jon Snow shows leadership with the men of the Night's Watch as their 998th Lord Commander. As contextual factors, such as follower readiness, defined as the ability and willingness to take on leaders' initiatives (Blanchard & Hersey, 1996), play an important part in leadership effectiveness, the leadership styles these two characters demonstrate might be different, but each one is successful in motivating followers to pursue their group's collective goals.

Research has identified a myriad of different types of leadership, some of which differ greatly from one another in terms of how they are enacted and their general effectiveness. Leadership types can be examined in at least three different ways: based on the leader's general style when making decisions, the leader's typical behaviors when interacting with followers, and the extent to which the leader engages in behaviors that motivate followers. A leader's decision-making style can range from completely giving away control to retaining full control. The daily behaviors that leaders demonstrate can be classified as being more focused on initiating structure, which prioritizes defining, structuring, and facilitating work, or consideration, which prioritizes respect, recognition, and mutual trust with followers (Fleishman & Peters, 1962). The motivational behaviors leaders can demonstrate typically fall into one of three types: laissez-faire, transactional, or transformational. As we will explore in this chapter, the characters fighting for the Iron Throne embody and demonstrate nearly every different leadership type, with results that range from abject failure to total success.

Decision-making Styles

When faced with making decisions, leaders can head in at least two directions. They can hold tight to their authority and make all decisions on their own without input from anyone, or they can fully relinquish control and allow their followers

Bend the Knee or Seize the Throne: Leadership Lessons from the Seven Kingdoms, 7–19
Copyright © 2023 by Nathan Tong and Michael J. Urick
Published under exclusive licence by Emerald Publishing Limited
doi:10.1108/978-1-80262-647-620231002

to make the decision they believe would be best for the group, typically within a set of criteria specified by the leader (Vroom & Yetton, 1973). The former is much like seizing the throne while the latter is more like bending the knee. While neither extreme of full control or full delegation is inherently good or bad, the optimal and most appropriate decision-making style for a leader to choose largely depends on the readiness of the followers. When followers are experienced, motivated, and capable of completing tasks on their own, leaders can, and should, bend the knee and allow them to make their own decisions that best serve the group and the group's goal achievement. However, if followers lack experience and/or are unable to execute tasks effectively without supervision (e.g., because of lack of motivation, lack of engagement, lack of commitment, etc.), then the leader should seize the throne and retain control of decision-making instead of giving that power and responsibility to their followers.

Leaders who allow their followers to make their own decisions are said be demonstrating delegative style (Gebert et al., 2010). The leader simply turns over the decision-making power and responsibility to followers, often after specifying certain parameters that must be met with the decision that is ultimately made. King Robert Baratheon exhibits this type of leadership throughout the first season. As a man who enjoys hunting, Robert often engages in the sport rather than spending time properly ruling his kingdom. He essentially abdicates his duties as king, delegating the decision-making responsibilities to his small council. (Robert's love of hunting ultimately causes his demise after an attack by a wild boar, although other factors such as drinking wine were involved.)

The other end of the spectrum of decision-making control is authoritarian style. Authoritarian style leadership is based on the notion that a leader should retain full decision-making control and makes decisions without seeking counsel from anyone, asking for anyone's input, or acknowledging any feedback (Kanwal et al., 2019). A leader who enacts authoritarian style does what they want, when they want, how they want, and followers are simply expected to carry out the leader's instructions. There are a variety of reasons a leader might engage in authoritarian style leadership. For example, a leader might be a tyrant who wants to maintain power and control at all costs, which drives them to exhibit authoritarian style decision-making. In other instances, the leader may be working with a newly formed team full of inexperienced individuals, whether it is, for example, a new team in a new organization or newly formed team in an existing organization. In cases like this, the leader may want to demonstrate authoritarian style decision-making, because asking for followers' input or delegating any decision-making responsibility to them may prove to be ineffective as the inexperienced individuals likely have neither the knowledge nor the insight to make decisions that will result in optimal results and outcomes.

In the series, Joffrey Baratheon exhibits authoritarian style leadership and quite literally seizes the throne. It is not because he is leading a new kingdom. Rather, Joffrey wants to maintain absolute control. As a new (and young) king, he believes that being the king means that he can do anything he wants and that others need to do whatever he says, no matter what. After assuming power and being coronated following the death of his father, King Robert, toward the end of the first season, Joffrey does as he pleases with both objects and people, often to the shock and horror of those around him. Perhaps Joffrey's most notorious use of authoritarian style of leadership is when he faces a decision regarding what to do about Eddard "Ned" Stark, who has been shackled in a dungeon awaiting his fate after threatening to expose Cersei's secret that her children were not fathered by Robert. Against the advice is his council, Joffrey decides to behead Ned Stark. This behavior goes against the counsel of his advisors, who caution him that Ned is beloved by the people and that killing him would not be a wise decision. However, with his authoritarian style leadership, Joffrey does as he pleases, completely ignoring the advice and input of those whose primary task is to provide him sound counsel.

Between these two extremes of delegative and authoritarian styles lie two additional decision-making styles: facilitative style (Fryer, 2012) and consultative style (Gillespie & Mann, 2004). In facilitative style, the leader participates in decision-making processes with the same amount of input and influence afforded to each and every member of the group. Facilitative style affords the group an opportunity to hear a variety of perspectives and to consider multiple factors introduced by group members before making the most optimal decision for the group, as a group.

This facilitative style of leadership can be seen in the way Mance Rayder leads the Free Folk, also known as the Wildlings. As a people, the Free Folk recognize no king, but that does not mean they wouldn't (or don't) respect a leader. In the show, it's told that Mance worked for many years bringing together different tribes to form the Free Folk, and for that he is named the King-Beyond-the-Wall. These tribes that make up the Free Folk all have different backgrounds, cultures, and rules; they speak different languages; and they were even previously in serious conflict with one another. However, Mance is able to unite them, creating a group so large that they pose a real threat to the Seven Kingdoms. Although Mance holds the title of King-Beyond-the-Wall, and the Free Folk respect him as their leader, his leadership style is facilitative. As their leader, Mance merely facilitates decision-making processes among the Free Folk. Certainly, they look up to him as he makes decisions about himself and his own fate, but what is never shown in the series is Mance taking it upon himself to make decisions for or about the Free Folk as a group.

The remaining decision-making style is known as consultative. In consultative style, leaders confer with followers, seeking their insight, input, and opinions. The leader then makes the decision on their own after considering the perspectives, responses, and feedback their followers have shared and expressed. Like with facilitative style, consultative style provides the opportunity for the decision-maker to consider multiple viewpoints before making a decision. Daenerys Targaryen often demonstrates a consultative style of decision-making. Before making her decisions, she almost always consults with Jorah Mormont, Missandei, and/or Grey Worm about how best to proceed. She seeks their advice and insight while also sharing her concerns with them. Another example of her consultative style is when she has a discussion with Tyrion Lannister and Lord Varys about her plan to attack King's Landing to remove Cersei from the throne.

Both Tyrion and Varys provide her with their input about why attacking King's Landing is not a good idea, primarily because she would end up slaughtering the people whom she set out to save. Later, Tyrion and Daenerys discuss again why attacking King's Landing is unwise, as it would result in the deaths of thousands of innocent people. Although Daenerys takes Tyrion's perspectives and input into consideration, she ultimately makes the decision to attack King's Landing. In this way, Daenerys's decision-making style is considered consultative.

Daily Interaction Behaviors

A second way to assess leadership is to evaluate the behaviors that a leader demonstrates while interacting with followers. Interactions with followers, especially when they are employees in a workplace, can be classified using two dimensions: initiating structure and consideration (Judge et al., 2004). Leaders exhibit initiating structure when their behaviors primarily focus on addressing or completing the task at hand and/or applying resources (e.g., manpower, time, materials) toward achieving a goal. Whether it entails planning, organizing, coordinating, incentivizing, or other similar task-focused behaviors, initiating structure is more concerned with getting work done and achieving goals than it is about showing care and concern for the person or people who are performing the work.

Cersei Lannister's leadership strongly exhibits elements of initiating structure. Any time she speaks with anyone, it is almost always strictly about how they are going to help her achieve her goal of taking and/or maintaining the Iron Throne. She rarely engages in conversations or interactions that stray from planning the generalities or details about her next move. Except for her conversations with her family, Tywin, Jaime, and Tyrion Lannister (her father, twin, and brother, respectively), she rarely ever expresses concern, support, or recognition with anyone she speaks to or with. And even when she talks with Jaime and Tyrion, her primary purpose for interacting with them is to advance her plan to rule Westeros.

In contrast to initiating structure, the other dimension of daily behaviors is consideration. Consideration occurs when a leader's behaviors demonstrate care and concern for followers, both at an individual level and at the group level, rather than focusing on getting work done. Leaders exhibit consideration when their behaviors show concern for followers' well-being, build trust, and engage with followers beyond what is necessary to complete work tasks. Demonstrating consideration can take many forms, such as asking an employee about their weekend or having a company barbeque, but its central focus is on the person or people performing the work, rather than on the work itself.

The leadership style of Olenna Tyrell, better known in the show as Lady Olenna, demonstrates many characteristics of consideration. She typically starts her interactions by asking about the person's well-being and showing concern for their livelihood. For example, when she invites Sansa Stark for a conversation in the garden (in an effort to extract information about Joffrey), she offers Sansa some lemon cakes because she knows they are Sansa's favorite. Although she has an ulterior motive of information gathering, Lady Olenna demonstrates consideration toward Sansa by not only offering her some cake to eat, but also by offering what she knows is Sansa's favorite flavor. After this display of consideration, Lady Olenna steers her conversations to more task-oriented topics (i.e., initiating structure), namely getting her granddaughter Margaery Tyrell seated on the Iron Throne by marrying Joffrey Baratheon.

Prior research has resulted in mixed findings about whether initiating structure and consideration are opposite ends of one spectrum or whether they operate independently from one another (Judge et al., 2004). In the first case, the argument that these two styles are on opposite ends of one spectrum means that a leader who displays more behaviors that initiate structure necessarily displays fewer consideration behaviors, and vice versa. In the other scenario, wherein these two types of behaviors are said to operate independently, a leader can be both high in initiating structure and high in consideration, low in both, or high in one and low in the other.

Almost none of the characters in *Game of Thrones* demonstrates pure consideration without any hint of initiating structure, likely because every character in the show has an agenda, whether it be seizing the Iron Throne for themselves or helping an ally to do so. Nonetheless, some characters demonstrate more consideration than others. Daenerys Targaryen, Jon Snow, and Lord Varys all exhibit consideration when working with others. They take the time to talk with those around them, making sure they feel alright physically and mentally, ensuring they have what they need, and generally asking about their well-being. As an example, when Daenerys first acquires Missandei, she immediately asks Missandei about her family and background while also making sure that she understands the dangers of going to war with her. Jon Snow demonstrates consideration with the men of the Night's Watch, and especially with Samwell Tarly. Sam is different from the other men; he is overweight, has poor eyesight, and is not as physically or (initially) mentally strong as the other men. Jon accounts for these facts when he works with Sam, making sure to give him the time, attention, and resources he needs to succeed. Lord Varys also shows consideration, which can be seen when he visits Ned Stark when he is imprisoned. Of course, he visits Ned to give and to get information (which is initiating structure), but he also brings Ned water, which is demonstrating consideration because he is looking out for Ned's needs and well-being.

The factors in your own work context will determine whether it is better to demonstrate more initiating structure or more consideration as a manager and/or leader. The most important factor to consider is the employees' characteristics, namely their readiness (Blanchard & Hersey, 1996), experience, and motivation, at both the individual and group levels. On one hand, when employees demonstrate readiness, have prior experience performing required tasks, and/or are motivated to perform, leaders can refrain from initiating too much structure and focus more on showing consideration. On the other hand, if employees are new(er) to their position or the organization, have little to no experience with performing the required tasks, and/or are not motivated to do their work, then the leader should initiate structure more than they should show consideration. Keep in mind, though, that purely initiating structure without showing any consideration can lead to disastrous results. Just look at the short reign of King Joffrey

Baratheon, who only initiated structure and showed absolutely zero consideration for his followers.

Motivational Behaviors

A leader without followers is simply an individual pursing a goal. What makes a leader a leader is the extent to which they can motivate others to willingly pursue a collective goal. Thus, a third factor to consider when assessing leadership is the leader's ability to instill a sense of motivation in their followers. Motivation can be thought of as the sum of someone's efforts. More specifically, motivation determines the direction, intensity, and persistence of one's efforts (Latham & Pinder, 2005). (See Chapter 10 for a more comprehensive exploration and discussion on motivation.)

These motivational leadership behaviors can be separated into at least three leadership types: laissez-faire leadership, transactional leadership, and transformational leadership. The first type, laissez-faire leadership, is characterized by the leader doing very little to actually lead followers. In fact, with laissez-faire leadership, the leader essentially avoids taking any sort of responsibility for what happens to, with, or among their followers. Laissez-faire leaders simply leave their followers to their own devices and primarily allow followers to make their own decisions and act on their own accord, as is done with delegative decision-making style. As discussed above, King Robert Baratheon largely delegates his leadership duties and responsibilities to others, primarily his small council. By doing so, Robert exhibits laissez-faire leadership. His behaviors demonstrate that his priorities do not lie in his role as leader and king of Westeros, but rather, his motivation is his pursuit of his hedonistic desires. He largely relinquishes and delegates his responsibilities as king to those around him, leaving important decisions and actions up to his small council.

However, laissez-faire leadership can sometimes be appropriate. For instance, if a manager in an organization is leading a team of seasoned, knowledgeable, and motivated employees, those employees do not necessarily need a leader who actively directs and controls the team, their decision, or their actions. The team knows what they need to do and will perform their tasks effectively and efficiently. The Army of the Unsullied is an example of a group that can operate efficiently with laissez-faire leadership. After the soldiers are fully trained, they no longer require an authority figure to supervise their every move, telling them what to do, when to do it, or how to do it. They are both willing and able to perform their duties to the best of their ability at all times.

The second type of leadership based on motivational behaviors is called transactional leadership, and it is perhaps the most ubiquitous type of leadership in modern organizations. As the name suggests, this type of leadership is like a transaction; there is a sense of "give something, get something." Typically, in transactional leadership, when a follower achieves a goal or otherwise does something correctly, they receive some type of reward. If they do not achieve a goal or if they do something incorrectly, then they receive some type of punishment or corrective action. In the workplace, this type of leadership might manifest as a regular paycheck for completed work, a bonus for completing a job under budget, or even a written warning for showing up late for a shift. In *Game of Thrones*, transactional leadership is consistently exhibited by Tyrion Lannister when he interacts with others. One of the family mottos Tyrion often states to others is, "A Lannister always pays his debts." This is the embodiment of transactional leadership. Those who interact with Tyrion perform tasks that he asks of them (i.e., they pursue a goal) because upon completion of their assigned task (i.e., goal completion), they will receive a promised reward from Tyrion or the Lannister family. Usually, their reward is gold or land, but it is always something of value, just like paychecks, bonuses, and avoiding disciplinary action are all items of value to employees.

Transactional leadership can be divided into at least two sub-types: management-by-exception and contingent reward. In management-by-exception, the leader only takes action to recognize followers' behaviors that are out of line with what is expected of them. Management-by-exception can be seen in the series when Arya trains with the man in the House of Black and White who calls himself "no one," although he bears the face of someone she met earlier who helped to protect her, Jaqen H'ghar. The goal of her training is for her to become one of the Faceless Men, a group of assassins who worship the Many-Faced God and are able to change their appearance at any time. Throughout their training, "no one" corrects Arya only when she performs incorrectly. He does not take the time or make the effort to recognize anything she does well, nor does he encourage her through his words and actions to perform better during her training. He only recognizes her behavior, and corrects it, when she makes a mistake.

The second subtype of transactional leadership is contingent reward, and research has shown it to be most effective form of transactional leadership (Waldman et al., 1990), in part because it is the most active. Contingent reward occurs when a leader promises and delivers some recognition or reward after the followers, either individually or collectively as a group, perform to an adequate standard. Unlike management-by-exception, which focuses on inadequacies and attempts to correct poor behavior with punishment, contingent reward encourages proper, adequate, and/or extraordinary performance by recognizing and rewarding those who exhibit expected and/or exceptional behaviors.

Contingent reward can be seen at the end of the series after Bran Stark is crowned the new King of the Six Kingdoms. In a display of contingent reward, Bran promotes the most effective individuals around him to his small council. Among these appointments is Tyrion, who is made Hand of the King because Bran has seen in him the behaviors required to excel in the role. When Grey Worm disagrees with this appointment, Bran states that Tyrion has done some bad things in the past and this role will allow (or force, depending on your perspective) Tyrion to make up for his past actions. Although it could be argued that Tyrion's appointment to Hand of the King serves a punishment for his past decisions and behaviors, the role actually comes with power and privilege. In that respect, Tyrion's appointment to the role can be seen as contingent reward rather than management-by-exception.

Bran also makes Samwell Tarly the Grand Maester because of Sam's demonstrated excellence in being knowledgeable about many subjects, particularly with history and science (as demonstrated in part by his dismissing Bronn's idea of rebuilding the brothels). In appointing this role to Sam, Bran recognizes Sam's extraordinary performance in (and love of) reading, history, and science. Bran also chooses Brienne of Tarth to be the Lord Commander of the Kingsguard and, in doing so, recognizes her demonstrated excellence in sword fighting and the bravery she consistently exhibits while in battle. The two other roles on Bran's small council assigned to those who are deserving because of their demonstrated abilities and excellence in their skills include Bronn as Master of Coin and Davros Seaworth as Master of Ship.

Transformational leadership, the third type of leadership, entails a leader being fully invested in each of their followers. Research suggests that transformational leaders demonstrate "the four I's," which are idealized influence, inspirational motivation, individualized consideration, and intellectual stimulation (Avolio et al., 1991).

All four of these elements can be seen in the way Jon Snow leads, which we will discuss in detail. The first of the four I's is idealized influence, and it centers around role modeling. Leaders who practice idealized influence behave as a role model for followers and, as a result, are trusted and respected by them. Jon Snow does this throughout the series no matter his situation. When he leads the men of the Night's Watch, he is consistently the first one to act, perform, or volunteer for whatever it is that needs to be done. He demonstrates idealized influence particularly well with Samwell Tarly. He is often seen showing Sam how to perform certain tasks and talking with him about why he makes certain decisions and takes certain actions with the hope that Sam can be more like him.

Inspirational motivation, the second of the four I's, describes how leaders spur followers to action. Followers then not only willingly put in effort to achieve goals, but they also strive to reach high(er) goals. This can be seen in Jon's interactions with the men of the Night's Watch as well as with the Free Folk. Neither side would have ever come together or accomplished what they did in fighting the White Walkers without Jon's inspirational motivation.

The third of the four I's is individualized consideration, and it occurs when a leader adjusts their behaviors to accommodate and/or address each follower individually in such a way that no two interactions are alike. Doing this makes each follower feel valued and demonstrates that the leader cares about each follower on a personal level. There is perhaps no clearer demonstration of Jon Snow demonstrating individualized consideration than in his interactions with Sam. He treats Sam differently from the other men of the Night's Watch, in large part because of Sam's needs, because of his poor eyesight, his timidity, and his less-than-ideal physical condition. As the series progresses, we see Sam become more confident, capable, and self-assured because of the way Jon's leadership accounts for Sam's specific needs.

Intellectual stimulation, the last of the four I's, helps followers challenge conventional thinking by encouraging and helping them to think new thoughts and adopt new perspectives, resulting in an expanded view of the world. Leaders who use intellectual stimulation generate creative thinking and innovation from followers. Jon Snow demonstrates this when he gets the men of the Night's Watch to agree to work alongside one of their adversaries, the Wildlings (the Free Folk), which would have never happened without Jon's leadership. Jon helps both sides to see and understand that they can accomplish more by coming together, and that doing so is the only way to survive an invasion from the White Walkers.

As these examples demonstrate, although the four I's are individual components, they can often work in tandem with one another. For instance, a leader's behavior that can be considered inspirational motivation might not be just inspirational motivation, but it can also overlap with intellectual stimulation.

Other Types of Leadership

There are other types of leadership that do not fall neatly into just one of the categories discussed above. Instead, they span across and build upon the best of each of the leadership assessment criteria discussed above. Recent research has shown that charismatic leadership (Conger et al., 2000) and servant leadership (van Dierendonck, 2011) styles transcend siloed criteria about decision-making control, daily interactions, and motivating behaviors. They have been shown to be effective leadership styles to employ when leading and motivating others.

Charismatic leadership can be seen when a leader displays characteristics that, to followers, seem larger than life. Research has found that charismatic leaders are set apart from "regular" leaders because the way they frame and communicate their inspirational and aspirational goals for themselves and their followers seem extraordinary (Conger et al., 2000). Although previous proposals claimed that charismatic leaders are born with their charisma, research has demonstrated that the traits charismatic leaders exhibit can be taught and learned (Antonakis et al., 2011). Among the traits seen as being charismatic are the use of metaphors and similes, stories and anecdotes, gesturing, and animated body language and tone of voice (Antonakis et al., 2011). Metaphors and similes help to invoke the use of symbolic language, which help in stimulating emotional responses from followers. Similarly, stories and anecdotes make ideas easy to understand and remember, in addition to helping followers identify with the hero of the story. The use of the physical self via gesturing, animated movements, and varying their tone of voice helps leaders to capture and maintain followers' attention.

However, researchers (e.g., Fiol et al., 1999) have also suggested that the context is important when considering how effective charismatic leaders can be. Specifically, organizational charisma relies heavily on the leader and their followers sharing the same set of values. Charismatic leaders are seen as being "larger than life" because of the characteristics attributed to them by their followers (Antonakis & House, 2002). In the series, Jamie Lannister embodies the notion of a charismatic leader. He killed the "Mad King," Aerys II Targaryen, earning him the nickname "King Slayer." This nickname alone makes him seem larger than life to others, especially to those who shared the same value of wanting the Mad King dead. However, it is Jaime's charisma, such as his use of stories and symbolic language, and his charm that elicit emotional responses from those around him and make them see him as a charismatic leader. Jaime's brother Tyrion is another good example of a charismatic leader. Tyrion demonstrates masterful storytelling, often weaving in similes and metaphors while speaking to compel others to see his point of view.

With servant leadership, the leader addresses the needs and wants of followers first before tending to their own needs. By doing so, they simultaneously develop their followers into self-sufficient and self-motivated individuals while also building strong relationships with each of their followers (van Dierendonck, 2011). What makes servant leadership distinct from other types of leadership is the leader's focus. Typically, with other leadership styles, the well-being of the group or organization is the leader's primary focus and/or overall goal. In contrast, servant leaders are genuinely focused on serving their followers (Stone et al., 2004). Because of this focus, one of the core characteristics of servant leadership is that the leader puts followers' interests above and ahead of their own (Greenleaf, 1977; van Dierendonck, 2011).

This commitment to nurture followers' interests can be seen in the way Daenerys Targaryen interacts with her followers. Daenerys' relationships with Missandei and Grey Worm exhibit servant leadership. Although Missandei and Grey Worm are actually both her servants, Daenerys builds strong relationships with both of them individually by demonstrating servant leadership. She is shown throughout the series as putting their needs first, prioritizing their needs to ensure that they are fulfilled. There is even evidence that, as a leader, Daenerys tends to the needs of those followers she does not even know personally. In one episode, her dragons burn and kill a goat farmer's entire herd. Instead of simply dismissing the farmer after he presents her with evidence, Daenerys fulfills his needs by restoring his loss and providing him with new goats so that he can continue to make a living. In the long run, Daenerys is not just tending to the needs of this one farmer; she is also taking action to sustain (or even improve) the livelihood of the people she is ruling. Another character who exhibits servant leadership is Lord Varys. Throughout the series, he often states that he does not serve any one house or one king but rather he serves the Kingdom of Westeros. He regularly repeats that "somebody needs to look out for the common people of Westeros" (i.e., him), and he consistently behaves in ways that reinforce that belief. He puts the needs of the kingdom before his own.

Leader–Member Exchange

One more theory about leadership that we would be remiss to leave unexplored is leader–member exchange theory (LMX). Since its introduction in the mid-1970s and early 1980s (Dansereau, et al., 1975; Liden & Graen, 1980), LMX has been widely validated and expansively explored by researchers. In a nutshell, what LMX theory proposes is that leaders have unique one-on-one relationships with each of their employees or followers (Graen & Uhl-Bien, 1995), as opposed to relating to all their followers as one giant collective unit. These one-on-one relationships might be of low quality, moderate quality, or high quality, and the quality of the unique bond that's formed between the leader and each of their followers depends on how they relate to one another (Graen & Uhl-Bien, 1995).

For example, a leader might develop a high-quality relationship with a specific employee because that employee is particularly competent at their job and they are eager to perform well, both of which are qualities that would likely draw the respect and admiration of the leader. In contrast, if there is an employee who is particularly lazy or unmotivated, produces sloppy or careless work, and/or typically just doesn't seem to be engaged or enthused about their job, there's a high probability that the leader's relationship with this employee would remain at low quality if (and often because) neither party wants to invest time, energy, or effort into enriching the relationship. In this type of situation, an effective leader would try to ameliorate the situation, rather than letting this employee continue to engage in subpar performance and/or produce poor-quality work. However, because there are multiple factors that impact every relationship (e.g., everyone has a different personality, motivation at work varies widely between people, time constraints, resource availability, etc.), there will be times when a leader has low-quality relationships with some employees, and the parties just accept that that's just how things are.

The manifestation of **LMX** theory appears throughout *Game of Thrones*. As a father and a leader, Ned Stark treats each of his children (and each of his subjects as Lord of Winterfell and Warden of the North) differently. When we are first introduced to the Stark family, it's made clear that Robb, Sansa, Arya, and Bran are Ned's "trueborn" children with his wife Catelyn. However, there are two other siblings in the family: Jon Snow and Theon Greyjoy. Jon is Ned's bastard son, who returns with him to Winterfell after Ned had fought in a war. Theon, on the other hand, had been taken as a ward by Ned. Through Ned's actions while he is alive, and via dialogue about him after his death, we discover that Ned loves all of them, but he has a unique relationship with each of them. The way he talks to each of them and the way he treats and interacts with each of them is similar, but each relationship is unique.

As an example, early in the first episode of the show, Ned sentences and executes a deserter from the Night's Watch. He brings Robb, Bran, Theon, and Jon with him to witness the execution (notice that he does not bring the girls). After Ned executes the deserter, he speaks privately and directly to Bran, explaining that the man who passes the sentence must also swing the sword to carry out the execution. This is a lesson he wants to teach Bran. It is unclear whether Ned thinks the other three sons already know this lesson he is trying to teach Bran about taking ownership and responsibility of one's decisions (we can assume he thinks they do), but what's important here is the unique dyadic relationship between Ned and Bran. Ned could have talked to all the boys as a collective group after the execution, but he chooses instead to talk to Bran individually. This behavior reinforces their relationship and further differentiates Ned's relationship with Bran from his relationship with his other sons (and daughters).

Another example of **LMX** is Jon Snow's relationship with Samwell Tarly. Jon has compassion toward Sam because of Sam's shortcomings (e.g., he is overweight, has poor eyesight, is meek and timid). The way Jon speaks to and interacts with Sam is completely different than how he speaks to and interacts with the other men of the Night's Watch. Especially after he is elected as the 998th Lord Commander of the Night's Watch, Jon is very assertive with the men. But with Sam, Jon consistently shows a level of compassion and understanding. He does not necessarily treat Sam any better or worse than he treats any of the other men; their dyadic relationship is simply unique. The same could be said of Jon's relationship with Maester Aemon. He treats Aemon with a certain level of respect and compassion that is markedly different from the rest of the men of the Night's Watch, but it is also a different kind of benevolence than what he uses with Sam. With each of these two men, Jon uses different words, vocal tones, physical postures, humor, and other characteristics, demonstrating that he has a unique relationship with each of them, and these two dyadic relationships are markedly different from how Jon interacts with others.

Other examples of very clearly differentiated dyadic LMX relationships in *Game of Thrones* include Daenerys Targaryen's relationships with Jorah Mormont, Missandei, Grey Worm, and Daario Naharis, and Tywin Lannister's relationship with each of his children, Jamie, Cersei, and Tyrion, along with many other dyadic leader–follower relationships in the show that are too numerous to name here.

However, as we can see in these examples and throughout the show, it is worth noting that LMX does not suggest that the leader changes who they are or that they put on a fake front for each of their follower. Instead, it is the leader's authenticity, and each follower's unique perception of the leader's authenticity, that helps shape the leader's unique relationship with each of their followers (Weischer et al., 2013). These perceptions can contribute to whether the dyadic relationship ends up being of high or low (or medium) quality.

Summary

We have discussed in this chapter that leadership comes in many forms, and each type of leadership has its merits and challenges.

- Sometimes, the situation a leader might find themselves in requires rigidity in how decisions are made and executed. In other words, they may need to "seize the throne." Other times, a leader's situation might require that they remain flexible and seek the input of their followers before any decisions are made and/ or before any actions are carried out. This can be viewed as "bending the knee."
- What researchers have found is that the "best" type of leadership is the one that considers the situation at hand (Vroom & Jago, 2007), which includes elements such as the decision(s) that need to be made, followers' ability and willingness to perform, and the leader's relationship with the followers, just to name a few.
- Organizational leaders and managers would do well to thoroughly consider these elements in their current situation to determine what leadership style and characteristics would be best suited to help them motivate their employees to achieve their collective goals.
- A leader's relationship with each of their followers is completely unique, and is based on not just the leader, but also on each follower's characteristics.

In this chapter, we have identified, defined, and explored different leadership styles and behaviors, determining that there is no one "best" leadership style. Sometimes leaders and managers need to seize the throne, and other times they need to bend the knee. However, one thing that is for sure is that leaders and managers have power. But where does power come from and how can it be best used to influence others? In the next chapter, we examine where leaders and managers can (and do) get their power from, how they can use their power to influence others, and how power can be abused.

Chapter 3

Power and Influence

There are many ways to define leadership, but implicit in most of these definitions is the concept of influence. For example, if leadership is viewed as a process of influencing others while resisting unwanted influence in turn (Daft, 2014), then it is clear that effective leaders must be good at exerting influence, which can occur no matter whether one seizes the throne or bends the knee. Influence can be defined as the ability or potential to affect someone or something (Merriam-Webster, n.d.). As leaders influence their followers, they are oftentimes trying to get them to "do" something in terms of taking specific actions for some specific purpose. That is, leaders want followers to move in a unified direction toward some individual or collective goal that (positively) impacts everyone in the organization.

There are many ways to build influence, but classic leadership theories suggest that having specific bases of power will help leaders to become more influential. In *Game of Thrones*, there are many characters who possess bases of power to influence others. This chapter considers how bases of power help leaders to build influence, how this influence can be effectively used, and ways in which power and influence can be abused. Throughout this chapter, we draw on examples of influence and power evident in characters in *Game of Thrones*.

Bases of Power

According to the classic research on influence by French and Raven (1959), there are several ways in which leaders can become influential. These are typically referred to as "bases of power" because these are foundations upon which leaders can draw to influence others. They include legitimate power, reward power, coercive power, expert power, and referent power.

Legitimate power is based on formal authority granted to an individual by the organization. It is related to one's title and position within a hierarchical structure. Individuals with this base of power are influential because they have direct reports or, in other words, they are someone's boss. A title can range from specific roles such as King or Knight in Westeros, to CEO or Manager in our own organizations. In *Game of Thrones*, Joffrey Baratheon is crowned King of the

Bend the Knee or Seize the Throne: Leadership Lessons from the Seven Kingdoms, 21–26
Copyright © 2023 by Nathan Tong and Michael J. Urick
Published under exclusive licence by Emerald Publishing Limited
doi:10.1108/978-1-80262-647-620231003

Seven Kingdoms after the passing of his father, King Robert. Though Joffrey is not well liked, people listen to him and do as he instructs, in large part because he possesses the title of King. Because people listen to his commands and carry them out, he is influential.

Reward power is based on a leader's ability to provide followers with things they need or want. This base of power relies on a leader's ability to provide others with something of value, or at least valuable to the follower(s), to become influential. In *Game of Thrones*, members of House Lannister are perceived to be wealthy and able to pay others well (including those to whom they owe debts). Because these followers assume they will receive their promised monetary rewards, the Lannisters are quite influential in the Seven Kingdoms. Tyrion Lannister in particular uses reward power on multiple occasions to get out of tricky situations. For example, his relationship with Bronn, who serves as his protector, is one based on the belief that Tyrion will pay him. At one point, Tyrion even tells Bronn not to betray him because he can pay more than the next highest bidder. Because of this, Bronn serves as Tyrion's champion in a trial by combat and goes to battle on behalf of Tyrion on multiple occasions.

Coercive power is basically the opposite of reward power. With this base of power, leaders have the ability to punish, penalize, or take away something desirable from followers. As such, followers often live in fear of their leaders and, to avoid negative consequences, do as they're told. Thus, this type of leader exerts influence in a manner marked by fear of the leader, or at least a fear of consequences. In *Game of Thrones*, there are many characters who exert influence through fear. Ramsay Bolton is perhaps one of the most despicable leaders who uses (and abuses) this base of power. He is known for torturing others, including Theon Greyjoy and Sansa Stark. While it seems that Ramsay gets pleasure out of these acts, he also bends Theon's and Sansa's wills to do his bidding, thereby influencing them out of their fear of physical pain.

Note that reward power and coercive power are separate bases. In organizations, leaders and managers can be given both types of power, but they may only have one type of power or the other. For example, a manager might be able to give an employee a written warning at any time for poor performance (coercive power), but they might not have the power to give an employee a raise, a monetary bonus, or a promotion (reward power), even if they feel that the employee is deserving. Going back to our example of Tyrion, he has reward power but not necessarily coercive power. Although he can pay people to help him, he does not necessarily have the ability or power to punish or penalize them if they chose not to accept his offers.

Expert power, the fourth base of power, results from a leader's ability to influence others because of their high level of skill or knowledge in some area. People who have expert power are typically influential because individuals in their organizations want them to be happy. After all, if they are unhappy, they might leave and take their expertise with them, to the detriment of the organization. An example of this in our own organizations would be the information technology (IT) people. Without their expertise, little work would get completed. In our own organizations, most of us rely on the "IT folks" when our computers and laptops stop working or don't do what they are supposed to do. This gives the people in the IT department expert power. Those with expert power might also be influential because they can teach others, passing on their skills, knowledge, and/ or perspectives. In *Game of Thrones*, Jaime Lannister is well known for his prowess in combat. After all, he is the one who killed Aerys II Targaryen, the "Mad King." Because of his high level of skill in combat, he is respected and followed by members of the Kingsguard and the Lannister army.

The final base, referent power, is about possessing a "likeability" factor. Leaders with this base of power create an emotive response among followers. That is, followers' feelings and emotions are positively activated by the leader, or even just the mere thought of them. These leaders are influential because followers willingly want to physically be around them, desire to be associated with them, and eagerly receive their perspectives. In *Game of Thrones*, Margaery Tyrell is briefly queen. Yet, she makes a big impact on people, especially on the citizens of King's Landing. Many of them love Margaery and are influenced by her because she is likeable, especially when contrasted with other royalty including Joffrey Baratheon and Cersei Lannister.

These are but a few examples from *Game of Thrones* of how characters in leadership roles grew their abilities to influence others. However, other characters who are also able to influence followers, such as Lord Varys, Jon Snow, and Daenerys Targaryen, draw from these five bases of power as well. These bases do not just exist in Westeros, though; they also occur in our own organizations. By recognizing what bases of power you possess at work (and developing those that you do not yet have) will help you become more influential in your own organizational context.

Effective Use of Influence

Obviously, throughout *Game of Thrones*, characters use power and influence effectively, as noted above by only a few out of many possible examples. What is often interesting, however, is that the bases of power can be interrelated and combined to be used together. For example, it is true that Joffrey possesses legitimate power because he holds the formal title of King. However, he is also feared due to his ruthless nature, having executed Ned Stark, abusing Sansa Stark, and murdering Ros with his crossbow, among numerous other atrocities. Thus, Joffrey uses coercive power to lead, in addition to using legitimate power.

Ultimately, though, Joffrey's leadership is unsustainable. Even in the fictional world of Westeros in *Game of Thrones*, which can be rather bleak, those leaders who abuse their power (including Joffrey, Ramsay, and Cersei) get their comeuppance and their influence and power are ultimately lost. Although these individuals possess and use multiple bases of power to lead, their influence does not last.

That said, those who have multiple bases of power that include expert power and/or referent power are typically more likely to be successful. Tyrion, for example, has reward power because of his family's wealth, but there is also something likeable about him. Thus, because some people (at least the viewers) seek to be around Tyrion, he also possesses referent power in addition to his reward power.

Likewise, Daenerys has the formal title of Khaleesi (legitimate base), provides rewards and punishments to her followers (reward and coercive bases), and is also likeable in the sense that others, such as Ser Jorah Mormont and Jon Snow, for a time, want to associate and be associated with her (referent base). She is one of the most successful leaders in the show as she rises to the role of Queen after being exiled for most of her childhood (at least until the coercive base takes over and she is removed from her role). Similarly, Jon Snow has expert power because he is good with a sword (expert base), gains legitimate power when he becomes Lord Commander of the Night's Watch (and is actually the true heir to the Iron Throne), and has referent power because others want to interact and be associated with him, making him a successful leader. Even though he is banished to return to the Night's Watch at the end of the series, he is still successful in the sense that he is not executed for killing the Queen and he can still exert his influence among the men at the Wall. Therefore, it would seem that those who possess referent power in addition to other bases of power tend to be the most successful in Westeros.

It is also worth noting that those individuals who possess multiple bases of power can use them in a way that incorporates servant leadership (Greenleaf, 1977). As we discussed in Chapter 2, this type of leadership focuses on the needs of followers. With servant leadership, leaders prioritize making their followers as successful as possible with the ultimate goal of improving a larger group of people, such as an organization or a society. Leaders who adhere to this approach are not self-serving and do not seek power for the sake of helping themselves. Rather, their use of their power is more concerned with helping others. (See Chapter 2 for a more thorough exploration of leadership.)

Jon Snow presents an excellent example of servant leadership used in conjunction with multiple bases of power. Above, we mentioned his referent base of power but also noted that, for killing the Queen, he is banished back to the Night's Watch. Even though he could have ruled the Seven Kingdoms (with or without Daenerys because he is the rightful heir), he chooses to engage in an act that some consider treasonous, in order to protect all the people of the realm. However, in doing so, he "lives to fight another day," so to speak, at the Wall.

The same high level of effectiveness can also occur when the bases of power are used with transformational leadership. This type of leadership focuses on the four I's (see Chapter 2 for additional details) and aims to make followers more self-sufficient and self-motivated (Avolio et al., 1991). As a reminder, the four I's are idealized influence, inspirational motivation, individualized consideration, and intellectual stimulation. As we examined in Chapter 2, Jon Snow demonstrates transformational leadership because he exhibits the four I's.

But, Daenerys Targaryen is another leader in the series who uses the four I's, making her a transformational leader. Like Jon, she uses multiple bases of power in conjunction with transformational leadership. As evidence of her effectiveness, consider the attitudes of the thousands of people she rules. They willingly act on her behalf. We can also quite literally see the transformations in Missandei and Grey Worm as the series progresses. They go from timid and obedient servants to empowered and confident followers who can think for themselves under Daenerys' leadership.

In *Game of Thrones* and in our organizations, it seems that those who possess multiple bases of power, as well as operate in a servant and/or transformational leadership manner, are likely to be more influential in the long term. Therefore, leaders should seek to develop multiple bases of power and operate out of the needs of their followers and the common good, rather than focusing on personal desires.

Abuses of Power

Of course, not everyone in Westeros uses their power for good, including Joffrey, Ramsay, and Cersei. In the real world, too, we can see abuses of power by leaders in our own organizations.

Abuses of power can take on several forms. One such form is that of bullying, which is the display of aggression, hostility, intimidation, or harm toward others (D'Cruz et al., 2018). Abuse can also take the form of various types of harassment including, but not limited to, sexual (Mainiero, 2020) and emotional (de Wet & Jacobs, 2020). Following from servant and transformational leadership theories, abuse would also likely occur when a leader places themself and their interests over the common good of others. Similarly, one must ask about how morally or ethically a leader uses their power to determine whether they are abusing it (more on this in Chapter 6 on ethics).

Each base of power has the potential to be abused. When power is abused, the negative consequences noted above will occur. Joffrey, for example, abuses his legitimate power stemming from his role as King. He executes Ned even after Ned confesses, he tortures Sansa, and he regularly threatens others. In each of these examples, Joffrey uses the influence that he has as King to drive fear into people or to punish those individuals he feels threatened by.

Reward power can also be abused. An example of this is the way the Lannister family says that they always pay their debts. This implies that they use their riches to achieve anything they want, which, of course, can be an abuse of power. Tyrion benefits solely for himself when he pays Bronn to protect him, for example. This could be considered an abuse of power because it is something not accessible to those who are less privileged.

Coercive power, which is when a leader is able to punish others or withhold positive outcomes from them, can also be abused. Sometimes this occurs by threatening someone or manipulating them by holding a negative outcome over them. Cersei does this when she forces Sansa to betray her father when she expresses her disappointment with Sansa and seemingly suggests that loyalty to her father is not befitting of someone who could be Queen of Westeros.

Expert power, derived from one's elevated level of skill or knowledge, can also be abused. Gregor Clegane, the knight also known as "The Mountain," for example, is highly skilled in combat. But he uses his physical prowess to bully and intimidate others, including shoving his brother Sandor's face into a fire when they were children, leaving Sandor permanently disfigured.

Referent power occurs when people want to associate with a leader because they have positive emotions toward that leader. As mentioned earlier, Daenerys possesses this type of power. One of the ways she convinces people to follow her (including Ser Jorah, Tyrion, Grey Worm, Missandei, Jon Snow, among many others) is because they like and respect her. However, she abuses this power when she asks her followers to destroy King's Landing, including numerous innocent denizens of the city.

In *Game of Thrones*, there are many additional examples of power being abused. In our own organizations, we can see abuses of power occur on a somewhat regular basis. When we find ourselves in leadership or management roles in which we leverage power, we want to make sure we regularly give ourselves reality checks. Are we using our power and influence for the good of all, or are we abusing it to make sure we get what we personally want, exclusively?

Summary

This chapter has explored leadership power, primarily focusing on the function of influencing others. We focused on the following concepts:

- Leaders can draw on a variety of bases of power from which they build influence. These can be related to a leader or manager's formal title, ability to reward others, ability to punish others, expertise/skill, and/or a positive emotional response in followers.
- Leaders who draw from several of these bases and use them in line with servant and/or transformational leadership approaches tend to be more successful in the long run.
- However, these bases can also be abused. Be careful when influencing others that you are using these bases to contribute to the common good and not your own personal needs exclusively.

Now that we have looked at power and influence possessed by leaders in *Game of Thrones* and our own organizations, we will turn our attention to leader emergence because in Westeros, even if someone is born into royalty, it does not mean that one automatically becomes a leader. And even if one does, it does not mean they will be leader for long. Look no further than Joffrey Baratheon's very short reign as evidence of this.

Chapter 4

Leader Emergence and Sustainability

The *Game of Thrones* television show, as well as Martin's original book series that it is based on, are influenced by the storylines, themes, and visuals of other fantasy authors. One of the most famous fantasy authors is J. R. R. Tolkien, and another book in this series focuses on his works set in Middle-earth (Urick, 2021). Tolkien had a lot to implicitly say about leadership and especially leader emergence. To paraphrase, he suggested that those individuals most suited for leadership roles may be the least likely to seek them out. In other words, the same attributes or behaviors that allow for leader *emergence* do not necessarily also predict leader *success*. *Game of Thrones* picks up on this theme from Tolkien and illustrates it over and over again throughout the series. Such a phenomenon is also supported by the trait theory of leadership.

However, the merits of the trait theory of leadership have been vastly discredited in recent decades (Collins, 2009; Judge et al., 2009). In essence, the trait theory suggests that successful leaders possess common sets of unchanging attributes that help lead to their effectiveness. Unfortunately, though, a clear list of such traits that lead to leader effectiveness has not materialized in the years following the articulation of trait theory. And, furthermore, other studies have argued that the importance of one's situation and other factors of a leader's environment may not allow for a stable list of traits to be effective (or ineffective) in all contexts.

Nonetheless, even though a stable set of traits that impact leader effectiveness has not been identified, what has been illustrated in research is that some traits or characteristics may predict leader *emergence* (Ensari et al., 2011). For example, the trait of extraversion, often characterized by how outgoing or audacious someone is, tends to predict leader emergence in Westeros as well as in our own workplaces, particularly in Western culture. In the Seven Kingdoms, Robert Baratheon emerges as king because he is outgoing in and about his attempts to overthrow the Targaryen dynasty and seize the throne. Take a moment to think about who gets promoted in your own organization. It is probably those individuals like King Robert who are actively vocal about wanting to take on a leadership role and make this desire known to those around them, rather than those individuals who remain quiet and/or do not speak up about or point out their own leadership

Bend the Knee or Seize the Throne: Leadership Lessons from the Seven Kingdoms, 27–31
Copyright © 2023 by Nathan Tong and Michael J. Urick
Published under exclusive licence by Emerald Publishing Limited
doi:10.1108/978-1-80262-647-620231004

qualities. Thus, extraversion is a trait that may lead to leader emergence, although it does not necessarily predict a leader's ultimate success, effectiveness, or sustainability. After all, King Robert's reign is quite short lived.

This chapter considers leader emergence. In doing so, we compare the characters of Cersei Lannister and Sansa Stark regarding how they rise to power, and we also discuss what specifically makes them sustainable (or not) as leaders. Following this comparison, other characters are briefly considered before analyzing leadership concepts related to emergence, sustainability, learning, and adapting.

Cersei Lannister

One of the most obvious illustrations of a character whose traits allow for her emergence into a leadership role, but not her success as a leader, is Cersei Lannister. Cersei is a character who greatly desires power but is not too well suited for it.

She first rises to power by becoming Queen of the Seven Kingdoms after marrying King Robert Baratheon. As she desires more and more power, she kills King Robert so that she is the only monarch on the throne and will raise her son Joffrey (who is not truly Robert's heir) to be king. As Ned Stark is onto her plan to retain power through the Lannister family line, she also finds a way to manipulate his image so that he is ultimately put to death.

Though she loves and is protective of her children, she also uses them for personal gain so that she would remain Queen (or at least Queen Regent) or so that her family name would stay in power on the Iron Throne. She seems to have little concern for what her children's desires are, such as in the case of sending her daughter Myrcella to Dorne, and driving a wedge between her son Tommen and his wife (and, thereby, Queen), Margaery.

Certainly, Cersei not only exhibits the trait of extraversion, but she also exhibits other traits as well that would predict her to emerge as a leader. She is cutthroat, competitive, and, above all, she is power-seeking. These traits, of course, allow her to emerge as the Queen of the Seven Kingdoms. In essence, her traits influence her behaviors. And, as such, she attains the role of Queen, mostly by killing those who oppose her or stand in her way.

Unfortunately, however, she does not necessarily have the support of those she rules. Those in the North, for example, openly lead an insurrection against her and her family. Even many of the denizens in the capital city of King's Landing apparently find her unlikable, if they aren't fearful of her. As seen in the show, they are more than happy to humiliate and jeer at her when she is forced to do a walk of atonement from the sept to the keep.

But ultimately, it is her personal traits that influence her propensity for violence, which ultimately end Cersei's reign. When she kills Missandei, she sets off unbridled anger in Daenerys, who has the resources (including a dragon) to bring Cersei's world literally crashing down around her. Fueled with rage, Daenerys does not care whom she kills after Missandei's execution and this, of course, includes killing Cersei, thereby ending Cersei's reign. Thus, the same characteristics and behaviors that lead to Cersei's rise to power not only do not lead to her success, but they also lead to her downfall.

Sansa Stark

Sansa Stark can be contrasted to Cersei in that she is both respected by others and able to emerge into a leadership role that will likely be more long term in nature than Cersei's. The reason for this is that her leadership is not based on unchanging personal attributes, as Cersei's is. Rather, Sansa's leadership is based on her using what she has learned from the variety of experiences she has lived through. These experiences help her to emerge into a leadership role (as Queen of the North), and she is more likely to be more successful in this role than Cersei is with hers.

In essence, Sansa has been through many leadership crucibles. A crucible is a vessel that heats metal at a high temperature so that it can be molded (Merriam-webster, n.d.). Applied in a leadership context, a leadership crucible is an event that is difficult, but one which provides an experience that leads toward personal development (Byrne et al., 2018).

Sansa certainly goes through many hardships in the series. She begins her journey in the series as a naïve idealist, which swiftly changes when she is mentally tortured by Joffrey Baratheon. Her father is killed in front of her after she is asked to turn on him. She is then forced to marry Tyrion Lannister and, without her consent, is shipped off to live in the Vale. She is subsequently abused by Ramsay Bolton after being forced to marry him. At the end of the story, Sansa is no longer a naïve idealist but, at the same time, she has also not given up on the world.

Her experiences, though tough, teach Sansa a lot. They make her strong and morph her into a pragmatic realist. She develops grit and has countless experiences to help her see and understand the types of behaviors that will work in a leader's favor and those that will not. She knows the harshness of the winter, how to line armor, and how to forge alliances. And during her crucibles along her journey, she builds a network of people who can help her to achieve her goals. She is thrust into a leadership role and ultimately succeeds in it. Furthermore, as someone who has been oppressed throughout the most recent part of her life, she has the wisdom to advocate for the secession of the North Kingdom from the Seven Kingdoms at the end of the series. These characteristics help make Sansa to not only emerge as a leader, but also to be effective as a leader and likely sustainable in her role.

Other Characters

Of course, Sansa is not the only character who is likely able to retain power. And, unlike Cersei, some characters are able to emerge into leadership roles because of their characteristics, and then retain their power because of them. Tyrion Lannister is an interesting example of this. Though he is presented as lusty and somewhat vulgar early on in the series, he evolves over time to be an effective leader, having helped stop Stannis Baratheon's advance on King's

Landing, as well as serving on the small council for multiple monarchs. But one positive trait that he possesses throughout the series, and that serves him well as a leader, is his desire to learn and obtain more knowledge. Another trait is his ability to negotiate well (see Chapter 9 for a more in-depth discussion on negotiation). Because of these personal traits, he learns about the stores of wildfire under King's Landing. And as a result of his ability to negotiate well, he is able to draw the Hill Tribes to his side, as well as to recruit Bronn as his personal swordsman and protector.

In addition to these traits helping Tyrion to emerge and be effective as a leader, they also complement his bases of power well, too (French & Raven, 1959). (See Chapter 3 for more detailed information about the bases of power.) For example, his trait of always learning and seeking new knowledge and information helps him to increase his expert power so that he is knowledgeable about many things. (After all, Tyrion himself said that that's what he does; he drinks and he knows things.) Tyrion's knowledge helps him to be successful in his role as a leader. Tyrion also possesses referent power, which helps him to be an effective leader. Tyrion is able to pass on his knowledge to others in an honest manner, such as in his discussion about what the Night's Watch truly is to Jon Snow. And his desire and willingness to always learn more, such as when he visits the Wall and travels with the Night's Watch, help him also to endear himself to others, thereby growing his referent power, leading to his effectiveness as a leader.

Speaking of Jon Snow, he is also someone who has leadership crucible experiences and emerges as a leader because of them. He also possesses referent and expert bases of power, which seem to become amplified after he is stabbed. This stabbing gives him new insight and it seems to provide him with a renewed spirit to fight for what is right. This causes people to rally around him to defend the North against the dead invaders. Furthermore, he also finds that he has legitimate power via his lineage as true heir to the throne. Though one could argue that he ultimately is not very successful because he does not stop Daenerys's destruction and is eventually banished North once again at the end of the series, it is not unlikely that he will again grow to lead the Night's Watch and be successful in his efforts.

As with the cases of Sansa and Tyrion, as well as potentially Jon Snow, these leaders are successful because they continuously learn over time and use their traits and bases of power in their favor, unlike Cersei. In the next section, we dive further into an analysis of leader emergence and success.

Learning and Adapting

When we consider leadership, it is important to consider both how leaders emerge and what makes them effective in their leadership roles in the long term. This idea has been explored quite a bit in leadership writing already, but one phenomenon that has been found is that those characteristics (including personal traits) that help leaders to emerge are not necessarily what make them successful (Goldsmith, 2010). Sometimes, traits and bases of power can help with both leader emergence and leadership sustainability, but it seems that in many instances, the most important factor in whether someone is an effective leader in the long term is whether or not they are able to learn and adapt.

Famous management author Peter Senge (2006) suggests that only those organizations that learn and adapt to their environment will survive. Applying this at individual level, it suggests that it doesn't matter what got you into a leadership role. Only by learning and adapting once you are in that role will you be successful in being sustainable as a leader. This seems true not only in Westeros but in our own modern organizations as well. Among the leaders in the series who continually learn and adapt are Sansa Stark (as discussed above), Jon Snow, and Tyrion Lannister. Each of them monitors their surroundings, pays attention to what is going on around them, and adapts their behaviors to suit what is happening to them and around them.

Summary

In *Game of Thrones* and in our own organizations, we see that the same traits or attributes that help an individual emerge into a formal leadership position do not necessarily predict their success in that role. This chapter has explored this phenomenon further, focusing specifically on the following:

- Traits and characteristics that help facilitate leader emergence can actually lead to one's downfall if they do not fit within one's changing environment.
- Leadership crucibles, in which an individual learns important lessons, can help a leader to be more successful in the long run.
- Successful leaders may possess traits and characteristics that fit their role, but they also possess bases of power that help them to be successful.
- Leaders will likely be more successful if they are continuously learning and adapting to fit their situation.

So far in this book, we have talked about different leadership styles, different bases of leaders' power and how these bases can be used to influence others, as well as a variety of characteristics and attributes that can predict leader emergence and leadership longevity. In the next chapter, we explore communication because communication is vital for leaders to convey their ideas, thoughts, and instructions to others. Without communication, leaders will not be able to express or share what they are thinking to get all their followers to work toward a collective goal.

Chapter 5

Communication

At first glance, the communication process seems relatively simple and straightforward, if we define communication as transferring meaning from one person to another (or multiple others). Note that we state *meaning* here instead of *information* because, as we will suggest in this chapter, meaning is created in part through the identities of the individual communicators.

Of course, quite a bit of communication occurs between the characters in *Game of Thrones* as well as within our own organizations. To be a successful leader in a particular context, you must be an effective communicator. Whether the message is given in a verbal speech, typed in an email, or written on a scroll and sent by a raven, communication between people is how thoughts and ideas get shared. This chapter provides examples of how learning from the interactions of the people of Westeros might help us to be more effective leaders in our own contexts by being better communicators. We begin first with a model of communication.

The Communication Process

The communication process seems to be pretty simple. Comprised of five steps (intent, encoding, transmission, receipt/decoding, and feedback; Krone, Jablin, & Putnam, 1987; Shannon & Weaver, 1964), the process suggests that information can move easily from one person to another. In the first step, intent, a communicator has an idea or a thought they want to convey. Next, in encoding, they try to represent the idea in some form (verbal, written, artistic, etc.). Then, in transmission, the communicator determines how to send that form to a receiver, such as in an online speech, via electronic media, speaking in person, etc. The receiver gets the message and interprets its meaning in receipt/decoding. Finally, in feedback, the parties determine whether the message that was encoded by the sender was received/decoded correctly by the receiver.

A hypothetical example of this from Westeros might be useful to illustrate these five steps. Let's say that Jon Snow wants to send a message about a Wildling attack to his sister Arya Stark (this step is intent). He chooses to write it down because that seems to be the most convenient way to get a message from the Wall to wherever Arya is (encoding). He writes his message on a scroll and gives it to a raven to

Bend the Knee or Seize the Throne: Leadership Lessons from the Seven Kingdoms, 33–37
Copyright © 2023 by Nathan Tong and Michael J. Urick
Published under exclusive licence by Emerald Publishing Limited
doi:10.1108/978-1-80262-647-620231005

deliver to her (transmission). This raven with the scroll finds Arya, and she reads and interprets the meaning of Jon's writing (receipt/decoding). Arya then sends an army to the Wall to help support the men of the Night's Watch (feedback).

This process seems easy enough, as there are only a handful of simple steps to complete it. However, there's a lot that could go wrong in this process, and there are multiple opportunities for the communication between Jon and Arya to break down. For example, Jon Snow might not have his ideas fully formed when he writes them on the scroll (e.g., because he is in a rush), resulting in the message being unclear or confusing to Arya. He may also not have the best handwriting, so Arya cannot adequately read or decipher the words, letters, or characters he has written. Also, maybe the raven gets lost, eaten by a dragon, or shot down by an arrow. Maybe the raven goes looking for Arya in Winterfell, but she has sailed away to Braavos. Or, possibly, Jon's letter includes references to people or places unfamiliar to Arya, so she does not understand the message. Lastly, even if Arya understands the message, she might not immediately send help, thereby denying Jon the feedback that she fully understood the message.

All these issues and more can occur when communicating, and such "noise" is not just a problem for antiquated styles of communication, such as using ravens. Indeed, communication breakdowns and barriers occur in our own organizations. Such issues include ineffective communicators (for instance, people who can't or don't articulate their thoughts and ideas in a clear manner that others are able to easily understand), choosing the wrong communication medium to transmit a message (e.g., verbally giving someone a reminder about an event or a meeting rather than sending a calendar invite), technology issues (e.g., when our Internet isn't working or we get locked out of our accounts), and unclear terminology or excessive use of jargon. We are sure that many readers have encountered such problems in their workplaces.

But noise is not the only issue with this particular model. In this simplistic view of communication, the relationship between the sender and receiver(s) is largely ignored. Thus, a more robust perspective on communication takes into account the relationship between the sender and receiver (Fairhurst, 2010). In our hypothetical example from *Game of Thrones*, for example, because Jon Snow and Arya Stark were so closely tied emotionally, it's likely they had inside jokes or references to places, people, events, and other things that only they would under-stand. If they were to try to use those same stories as points of reference to others outside of their relationships, others might not "get" them. That is, there would be a complete lack of understanding. Additionally, Jon would also likely verbally speak to Arya differently than he would with others, such as Ned and Catelyn Stark (his adoptive parents) or his superiors in the Night's Watch. In other words, relationships matter when considering what the message is, how to craft (i.e., encode) the message, and how to decode the message.

Fairhurst's Types of Communicators

The work of Gail Fairhurst points out the importance of relationships in the communication process. And it is also important in analyzing a communicator's style. One way to categorize types of communicators that may be helpful to leadership studies is to group them into three styles: expressive, conventional, and strategic (Fairhurst, 2010; O'Keefe & McCornack, 1987).

Someone with an expressive style tends to say (or write) what they think. In other words, they speak their mind. A positive characteristic about this style is that this person is open and honest. In fact, this openness is part of the charm of a leader with this communication style. Some people gravitate toward this individual because they are perceived as a "straight shooter" who will provide honest information and feedback. As a negative, though, this person might also be perceived as rough around the edges and not knowing their audience when they communicate. They may not necessarily filter their thoughts before they speak, which can potentially lead to problems.

Ned Stark is a typical expressive. He is well liked because he is perceived to be honest. Yet, his honesty gets him into some pretty bad situations, such as when he openly tells Queen Cersei and Petyr Baelish that he believes Joffrey to be illegitimate in inheriting the Iron Throne and plans to remove him from the throne. His inability to craft his message to better suit his audience limits his longevity as an influential leader in Westeros.

A conventional communicator does what they believe is most appropriate in a situation. This type of leader conveys to constituents what they think they want to hear. This can be a bit problematic, especially if the message that a leader with conventional communication style provides to different groups is contradictory in nature. They might rephrase a sentiment from one group to another and, in the process, inadvertently change the meaning of the message.

Petyr Baelish could be considered an example of a conventional communicator. He is very influential in the Seven Kingdoms, in part, because he tells others what they want to hear. To their faces, he flatters Cersei and Joffrey, despite working against them in the shadows. Likewise, his message to Sansa Stark is that he is helping her escape from the Lannisters, yet he delivers her to Ramsay Bolton, who is arguably just as evil as Joffrey. He also makes Ned Stark believe that he is on his side, but he ultimately betrays Ned. However, Petyr's conventional communication nature eventually catches up with him. Delivering contradictory messages, two-timing others, and selling out those he influences eventually lead to his death in Winterfell.

Finally, a leader with a strategic communication style has a heightened sensitivity to language, and they use it in a way that the messages they send resonate with multiple parties. Strategic communicators see a variety of possibilities in the way that they communicate, and they try to work toward goals that are valued by multiple people.

We would argue that Jon Snow is a leader with strategic communication style. Jon's communication is crucial in defending the Wall against the Wildlings (who call themselves the Free Folk). Yet, he is also able to communicate with the Free Folk in such a way that they accept him. By bridging these two diverse groups that are sworn enemies, Jon Snow is able to unite the Night's Watch and the Free Folk toward a vision that helps protect Westeros from a greater enemy, the White Walkers. Of note is that although Jon's fate is arguably not an exceedingly positive one, he is one of the few characters who survives from the beginning of the series through to its end, in part because of his strategic communication style.

Ethical Considerations

Of course, there are some ethical considerations that must be explored when examining a leader's communication style. For example, many ethical frameworks (see Chapter 6 for a fuller discussion on ethics) would suggest that it's necessary for leaders to craft a message that is truthful. Others, however, might suggest crafting a message that gets specific results regardless of whether or not it encompasses an honest, complete, and transparent representation of facts.

Some of the communication types noted above might be more in line with certain ethical perspectives than others. For instance, expressives are typically noted to tell the truth (or at least their perspective on what they believe the truth to be), while conventionals and even strategics may appear to be more manipulative in nature regarding how they spin a message to fit certain audiences.

As an example, Tyrion Lannister could be considered strategic in his communication. He is able to influence the Hill Tribes to fight alongside the Lannisters and defend King's Landing, he convinces Bronn to be his champion when he is imprisoned in the Eyrie, and he publicly criticizes King Joffrey and lives to tell the tale. At the end of the story, like Jon Snow, he is one of the few characters who lives through the entire events of the series. And he is in a formal leadership role as the Hand of the King to King Bran Stark. Through it all, Tyrion influences others and makes decisions – including those who save their lives during the Battle of King's Landing – and so he should also be considered to be a leader.

But can we consider Tyrion an ethical leader? Depending on your ethical model, you might believe that Tyrion's penchant to focus on his own personal benefit early in the story to not be ethical. As a leader, should he focus instead on how to benefit a collective group, as several ethical models would suggest? While others might argue that, by the end of the tale, Tyrion does indeed work for the good of others, his character progresses down this path as the story continues.

Nonetheless, the point of this discussion is not to debate how ethical or not Tyrion and other characters in *Game of Thrones* are in this chapter (exploring ethics is for another chapter in this book, after all). Rather, the point is to suggest that there are some ethical considerations to think about when we analyze leaders' communication styles. How often do (or should) leaders tell the complete, unadulterated truth? Do leaders tend to speak plainly or in metaphors, and when should they do so? What is the most appropriate style of communication in a particular leadership context: expressive, conventional, or strategic? What is the most appropriate style of communication for you in your organizational context?

Summary

Leaders in *Game of Thrones* communicate in a variety of ways. Some of these approaches to communication are successful in the long term, while others are not. This chapter has examined communication in *Game of Thrones*, offering the following points:

- Though simple in nature, the communication process of intent, encoding, transmitting, receipt/decoding, and feedback is actually quite complex because noise can occur anywhere throughout these steps, and communicators must consider the relationships they have with their audience.
- Three types of communicators are expressive, conventional, and strategic. Though each style has advantages and disadvantages within particular contexts, those leaders who can speak to multiple audiences may be the most effective.
- There is an ethical element to communication. Regardless of what communication style a leader uses, their followers will likely want honest and truthful communication. Spinning a message in such a way that it distorts its meaning or to use it exclusively for personal gain may not lead to sustained leader success.

As we just discussed, ethical considerations are important to keep in mind when thinking about a leader's communication style. Fortunately, the next chapter delves more deeply into ethics. Any time there is an interaction between two or more people, there is almost always a gray area about the appropriateness of people's behaviors and how they treat one another (or multiple others). This gray area is what is referred to as ethics.

Chapter 6

Ethics

This chapter begins by examining theories related to how leaders draw upon different ethical frameworks as they engage in decision-making and illustrates them through decisions made by characters in *Game of Thrones*. We then consider ways that leaders might also use these theories to inform their own decisions. Of note, this chapter draws heavily on the ideas initially published in a 2017 article from the *Journal of Leadership and Management* by Michael Urick and Nicholas Racculia.

Leadership and Decision-making

There are certainly many factors that could impact the decisions that leaders make, but a leader's personal set of values is one crucial consideration for the choices they make, such as whether to seize the throne or bend the knee. Decision-making has been studied in leadership and management research for decades. An interesting area that researchers have explored concerns contextual constraints that limit the ability to make a perfect decision (Child, 1972). This stream of research proposes that leaders exhibit bounded rationality—meaning their decisions are logically limited (Staw & Ross, 1987). Pure rationality assumes that decisions are made without being influenced by one's emotions, with all the resources necessary to fully understand and implement a decision, and with perfect information (i.e., no information is missing or unobtainable). Of course, these assumptions are all incorrect because we know people experience emotions, resources (e.g., time, money, property) are almost always limited, and perfect information is almost impossible to get, thereby making the case for bounded rationality.

With regard to leaders possessing imperfect information, there are several biases that influence their collection and interpretation of the information that they do have access to, and that they use to make decisions. For example, bounded rationally can exist in part due to a leader's unrelenting commitment to a course of action (Staw, 1976, 1981; Staw & Ross, 1978, 1987), which may be strengthened by the level of responsibility they feel for a decision's outcomes, the feedback they are given about their decision (Barton et al., 1989), and their attitude toward accepting risk (Kahneman & Tversky, 1979).

It is possible that leaders may be committed to particular choices because of their comfortability with particular ethical decision-making frameworks they use

Bend the Knee or Seize the Throne: Leadership Lessons from the Seven Kingdoms, 39–44
Copyright © 2023 by Nathan Tong and Michael J. Urick
Published under exclusive licence by Emerald Publishing Limited
doi:10.1108/978-1-80262-647-620231006

to make their decisions. Likely, the chosen framework closely fits with their world-view. This is one reason why it is necessary to consider a leader's values as we consider the decisions that they make.

Ethics and Decision-making

The field of ethics helps evaluate decisions on the basis of whether they are morally right or wrong. One model for how leaders might leverage ethics while engaging in decisions suggests that there are four steps to making choices: moral awareness, moral judgment, moral commitment, and moral behavior (Rest, 1986; Trevino & Nelson, 2007). Moral awareness occurs in the first step. This is when leaders are faced with a choice to make, and they recognize that there are moral implications for their situation based on the decision they make. If a leader or their close confidants care about issues of morality, that leader is more likely to perceive most choices as having moral components, which then requires them to use their values to help them guide their decision-making. In other words, the decision they make should align with their personal values.

The second step of this model is moral judgment. This step is when leaders decide how they should confront the decision(s) with which they are faced. Their approach will likely depend on their level according to Kohlberg's Theory of Cognitive Moral Development (1969). Leaders in the post-conventional level will resolve (or at least try to resolve) every ethical issue consistently by using an ethical decision-making framework. However, those who are in the conventional level will follow along with social norms while those in the pre-conventional level seek to avoid pain. Because many of the characters in *Game of Thrones* appear to be in the post-conventional level, and because this label may be best for leaders to deliberately consider their values in the choices that they make, we focus on this post-conventional level as we present ethical frameworks below.

But before we explore the frameworks, let's finish discussing the stages first. Moral commitment is the third stage of the ethical decision-making model. Here, a leader contemplates how much (or how little) they care about what they "should do" in the situation given their individual level of moral development and chosen framework from the previous stage. If they care about the problem they are confronting, then they will be dedicated to pursuing what they believe to be a moral choice. Of course, if they truly are not concerned with their problem, they will not be dedicated to what they should do, even if they understand it to be moral.

The last stage of the ethical decision-making model is moral behavior. Put simply, this is the follow-through where decision-makers actually implement their choice based on the previous stages, informed by the earlier stages. As we have introduced the concept of ethical decision-making frameworks, we will now explore a few of these in the next section.

Ethical Decision-making Frameworks

There are a number of ways leaders can make decisions based on certain frameworks that draw on particular values (Wilkens, 2011) within the post-conventional stage of Kohlberg's theory (1969) noted above. Below are a few example frameworks upon which leaders can draw. It should be noted that there are similarities and differences between each distinct framework.

The first type of framework focuses on principles that are universal to everyone regardless of context. Kantian ethics is a decision-making framework which suggests that leaders have duties they must follow. These duties that guide their choices are derived from a reflection of what the world would be like if everyone engaged in such behavior. A categorical moral imperative emerges when a leader can answer that such behavior would improve the world. Likewise, virtue ethics suggests that there are principles that are the same for everyone but that these emerge as a result of good character traits. Thus, from this framework's perspective, moral decisions come from a package of virtues (such as a leader who simultaneously possesses courage, wisdom, and generosity all together). A virtuous individual is one who uses multiple virtues to make decisions consistently over time.

A second type of framework focuses on the outcomes of decisions. Egoism may not necessarily be viewed as "moral" by many readers, but it is a framework based on particular values that guide decisions, so it is included here. This framework suggests that decision-makers rationally make choices that benefit themselves in the long term. Utilitarianism might be more in line with readers' expectations of ethical frameworks. Like egoism, this framework also focuses on outcomes, but it suggests that good decisions are those that lead to the greatest happiness for greatest number of people.

A third type of framework considers the context in which choices are made. Though not initially formulated as an ethical model, behaviorism suggests that leaders engage in behaviors because they are exposed to strong stimuli that occur in their environment. Cultural relativism, similarly, is a framework which suggests that decision-makers make choices that fit within the social norms of the cultural environment in which they find themselves.

The final type of framework considered here leverages religious values. Though various religions around the world possess different values (and, likewise, the religions of the people of Westeros are fictional and different than our own), there are some common moral considerations that typically exist across many faiths. For instance, acting out of love or respect to others may be a common value held by many faiths, and this is consistent with the situation ethics framework. Likewise, natural law ethics is a framework derived from a theological basis that simply suggests leaders use their conscience to make decisions. Lastly, divine command theory is an ethics framework that suggests decision-makers turn to explicit religious texts and teachings as they make their choices.

Of course, there are other ethics frameworks that can be used for decision-making, and these may be oversimplified representations of values. Yet, these frameworks are useful in clarifying how leaders make decisions. You have likely seen people use these values to make decisions in your organizations, and they can also be seen in *Game of Thrones*. The next section highlights how these frameworks are used by various characters in *Game of Thrones* to further clarify and explore these frameworks through examples.

Decision-making Examples from *Game of Thrones*

In *Game of Thrones*, several characters appear to operate in the post-conventional stage as they steadily leverage specific values highlighted in some of the particular ethical decision-making frameworks discussed above.

The first character considered here is Eddard "Ned" Stark, Warden of the North before he is named Hand of the King by Robert Baratheon. He is chosen for this role because of his consistency, loyalty, and honor, adjectives which many of the characters use to describe him throughout the show. Many of the decisions Ned makes show evidence of characteristics of both Kantian ethics and virtue ethics because they focus on those truths that he views to be universal. In agreeing to be the Hand of the King, Ned believes that he has a duty to his friend Robert. He also attempts to be honest, another moral duty, in trying to determine who should be the true heir to the throne, as we see in the first season of the show. As he follows these duties and faithfully executes them, he also shows courage and perseverance, both of which are in line with virtue ethics.

The second example is King Robert Baratheon. Leading a rebellion against the prior king benefited Robert personally because he became the king as its outcome. While being king, Robert enjoys personal gratification and delegates much of the rule of Westeros to others, likely because he does not enjoy that part of the role. Examples of the choices he makes include gluttony in overeating and drinking to excess, engaging in many extramarital sexual relations, and hunting. Thus, Robert regularly makes choices that increase his personal enjoyment while not concerning himself with others. With almost every decision he makes, whether getting drunk off wine or suiting up for a tournament, Robert hopes to benefit himself by having fun, which seems in line with the egoism framework.

On the other hand, Lord Varys is also concerned with outcomes, but his attention is focused on the greater good of the realm rather than his own personal outcomes, which seems very much in line with the utilitarianism ethics framework. Throughout the series, Varys states that he serves the population of the Seven Kingdoms, as opposed to any one ruling house or monarch, and seeks to benefit the entire realm. This focus impacts more people positively than simply serving one noble family or king (or himself) exclusively. For example, Varys helps Tyrion escape from imprisonment, conspires against King Joffrey, competes for power with Petyr Baelish, and imprisons a sorcerer in a box. At face value, these choices and their resulting actions seem very questionable, yet through the lens of utilitarianism, the outcomes are all that matter and not the means Varys takes to achieve them. With each of these choices, Lord Varys suggests and believes that the results will promote a more, if not the most, positive and pleasurable state for others.

Stannis Baratheon is King Robert's brother, and he firmly believes that he should be the next ruler to be placed on the Iron Throne after Robert's demise. Like Lord Varys, he is also focused on outcomes in terms of the behaviors he engages in, but, unlike Varys, he does not necessarily believe that he is completely in control of his environment. As he wages a war to claim the kingdoms, Stannis consistently mentions fate and truly believes that he is destined to rule. In line with behaviorism, Stannis is confronted with stimuli that guide his actions, including receiving a raven from Ned Stark about the death of Robert and being spurred on by his supporters, especially Melisandre, one of his advisers who constantly reassures him that ruling the Seven Kingdoms is his destiny.

Jon Snow also considers context in his decisions, though his approach is more consistent with cultural relativism. Being a bastard, Jon is an outsider in his home at Winterfell, though he follows their customs. Similarly, Jon follows the rules of the Night's Watch when he pledges to their order. However, when he is captured by the Wildlings, he ultimately adopts some of their norms and even eventually welcomes them to live with the men of the Night's Watch at Castle Black.

Cersei Lannister's decisions seem to be in line with situation ethics. In her choices, she often protects her children, such as taking measures to protect them when she believes that her city will be sacked. Likewise, she asks Jaime to rescue her daughter from a family that she believes may be a threat. As situation ethics emphasizes distributing care, Cersei prioritizes such "love" to her children, even if her decisions do not benefit others.

It is perhaps more difficult to label Daenerys Targaryen's ethical framework, but we would argue that it contains elements of natural law ethics (even though her ultimate decision toward the end of the series may not be in line with this framework due to the destruction it caused). Yet, we would suggest that in most of her choices, she seems to follow her conscience, which allows her to emerge as a leader. Many of the choices she makes based on her conscience include freeing slaves, chaining up her dragons when they become a threat to others, and getting engaged to someone for the sake of creating peace.

Finally, Melisandre is known by some characters as the "Red Woman" in her role as counselor to Stannis Baratheon. Almost all her decisions are guided by the divine command theory framework. She advises Stannis to make decisions and engage in actions that are communicated directly to her through the fire, which is a representation of her faith's deity. She understands right and wrong based on visions she sees in fire, which tell her what decisions and resulting actions are appropriate. As she receives these visions, she advocates that Stannis burn nonbelievers, sacrifice his daughter, and engage in a major sea battle.

Ethical Frameworks in Organizational Contexts

So far in this chapter, we have considered examples of a few values-laden frameworks evident in *Game of Thrones*. By the end of the series, many of the characters noted above see tragic outcomes that are not what they intended as a result of their decisions and actions (indeed, only a few of them are still alive at the end of the series). Even so, each of these characters is so committed to their decision-making paradigm to the point that they ignore other options for how to engage in the decisions and choices they face. This indicates a challenging conundrum for leaders: how should decisions be judged? Are "good" decisions solely those that have positive outcomes, leverage certain values, and/or are driven by particular motives? Likely, each person reading this book will answer these questions differently, but they are worth contemplating as we consider our own decisions we make in our own leadership roles.

In our leadership roles, we must further acknowledge that the types of decisions we make may not be effective throughout our time as leaders. It is likely, for example, that the choices people make that enable them to emerge as leaders will likely not help them be successful in their roles as leaders (Shamir & Howell, 1999). For example, Cersei Lannister's situation ethics approach, in which she prioritizes her children, could not sustain support from her followers because she does not read the changing signs of her environment in King's Landing.

We also must consider that others, namely followers, may not have the same set of values as a particular leader and will therefore not always agree with that leader about whether a decision is positive or negative. We see this through the discrepancies that exist between the varied values of the characters in *Game of Thrones*, such as with the Lannisters. Consider that Tyrion Lannister kills his father Tywin. At its core, this killing is the result of a divergence between Tyrion's values and Tywin's decisions and actions. However, these discrepancies also occur in our own organizations. For example, we may generally agree with our supervisor on most things, but there may be times when our values diverge from those of our supervisor. Yet, understanding different perspectives, even if we do not agree with them, can perhaps lead to fruitful and productive discussions of the variety of approaches people can take in making decisions. It may very well also promote greater understanding of diverse ideas in organizations without demonizing those who possess a different perspective than our own, or that of the majority. This, in turn, could help reduce unnecessary disruptive conflicts in our organizations, such as killing a leader you disagree with, like Tyrion.

Summary

A number of characters in *Game of Thrones* highlight various types of ethical decision-making frameworks. This chapter has explored the following:

- A consideration of ethics is fundamental to leadership because values help inform the decisions leaders will make as part of their role.
- Leaders may be guided to minimize pain, to conform to a group's standards, or to leverage particular decision-making frameworks.
- Some decision-making frameworks include those focused on universal principles, the outcomes of a decision, the context in which a choice is made, or faith-based considerations.
- Many characters in *Game of Thrones* have leveraged each of these different frameworks in their decision-making, as have leaders and other colleagues in our own organizations.
- As leaders, we must reflect on how to judge good decisions from bad, and what to do when we possess different values than others in our organization.

Typically, it is only when leaders' and managers' decisions and actions are deemed ethical that employees are willing to accept, follow, and execute those decisions and actions. But even when these are perceived as ethical, employees still need to be motivated in order to carry them out to the best of their ability. In the next chapter, we explore the determinants of motivation so that, as a leader, you're able to motivate your followers.

Chapter 7

Motivation

Organizations can only function effectively when their employees perform the work they are supposed to perform. For better or for worse, the work that employees carry out on a daily basis can vary from doing the bare minimum to going well above and beyond what's required. What determines each employee's demonstrated or actual level of performance is their motivation. In this chapter, we explore what motivation is, what some of the elements of motivation are, and what determines motivation. In *Game of Thrones*, each character has their own motivation for their behaviors, including when to bend the knee to others or when to take charge by seizing the "throne." Similarly, in our own organizations, everybody has their own motivations for their behaviors, and those motivations can ebb and flow.

Defining Motivation

Think back to the last time when you felt really motivated to work on or complete some task, such as your favorite hobby, an assignment at school, or a project at work. What did it feel like internally for you? Were you excited? Raring to go? So focused on what you were doing that you lost track of time? And what external factors were present that motivated you? Was there a reward to be won? Was there recognition to be earned? Was there a deadline that needed to be met? Whether internal or external, there are numerous factors that can and do motivate people to make progress toward an end goal or complete whatever task they are working on.

Motivation is defined as a set of internal and external forces that drive an individual to take specific actions to reach a goal, while determining the intensity and persistence of their actions and efforts (Latham & Pinder, 2005). In other words, motivation is the driving force behind producing and sustaining goal-focused behaviors. Motivation that stems from internal factors or simply from pleasure in performing a task is referred to as intrinsic motivation (McAuley et al., 1991). Examples of intrinsic motivation include feeling a sense of enjoyment in performing an activity, experiencing personal fulfillment or a sense of accomplishment, engaging in self-expression, or learning new knowledge or mastering a new skill simply for the sake of learning something new and/or different.

Bend the Knee or Seize the Throne: Leadership Lessons from the Seven Kingdoms, 45–50
Copyright © 2023 by Nathan Tong and Michael J. Urick
Published under exclusive licence by Emerald Publishing Limited
doi:10.1108/978-1-80262-647-620231007

In *Game of Thrones*, almost nothing is more important for Brienne of Tarth than maintaining her honor and her word. Throughout the series, she demonstrates via her words and her actions that she is intrinsically motivated to do everything possible to maintain her honor and fulfill her obligations. For instance, during her time transporting Jamie Lannister and when she protects Sansa Stark, she is motivated by her promises and commitment to Catelyn Stark, even after Catelyn's death. Arya Stark is another character who demonstrates intrinsic motivation. After being separated from her family and then watching her father Ned get beheaded, she creates a mental note of all those who have wronged her and her family. Killing all those on her list is the intrinsic motivation that fuels Arya's decisions and behaviors throughout the series.

Motivation that comes from outside of oneself is called extrinsic motivation (Galbraith & Cummings, 1967). External factors that motivate people typically involve gaining something of value, preventing the loss of something valuable, and/or avoiding the introduction of something unwanted. For example, employees in organizations might be motivated to work hard because they can gain something valuable, such as a monetary bonus, the opportunity for promotion, or recognition from management. They may also be motivated to do their best work to prevent losing something valuable, such as their preferred work schedule, their benefits, or even their employment. Lastly, employees can be extrinsically motivated to perform their work properly because they want to avoid an unwanted outcome, such as being verbally chastised by their peers or formally reprimanded by their supervisor.

Through all her decisions and behaviors in *Game of Thrones*, Cersei Lannister shows she is extrinsically motivated. Her goal in the series is to maintain her grip on the Iron Throne, and she directs all her decisions and actions toward achieving that goal. Every word she speaks, every action she takes, and every decision she makes all work toward her goal of remaining Queen (or Queen Regent) of the Seven Kingdoms.

Another character who exhibits extrinsic motivation is Petyr Baelish. Nearly everything he does is to help himself to achieve one of two goals: to earn more wealth or to get closer to the Iron Throne. His actions and decisions are not typically done to make him feel fulfilled or to give him a sense of accomplishment (at least not unless that accomplishment is sitting on the throne as king). Instead, there is consistently something to be gained for Petyr. For instance, when he takes Sansa Stark under his wing and offers her protection, he is not doing it out of the kindness of his heart, which would be intrinsic motivation. Instead, he does it to try to earn favor from House Stark or to benefit himself in some way.

As a final example, Tyrion Lannister typically tries to offer extrinsic motivation to get others to act. Instead of appealing to others' hopes and desires to motivate them (which would be intrinsic motivation), Tyrion offers them extrinsic motivation in the form of money or land. When he is held prisoner in the sky cells in the Eyrie, he tries to motivate Mord, the dim-witted guard, to release him by offering him gold. (It didn't work.) Using the same tactic of offering gold as extrinsic motivation, Tyrion also tried (and succeeded) to motivate Bronn into serving has his personal swordsman and guard.

Determinants of Motivation

Research has shown that motivation determines three elements of people's efforts: the direction of their effort, the intensity of their effort, and the persistence of their effort (Latham & Pinder, 2005). The direction of one's efforts establishes what they are going to focus their energy on. In the workplace, an employee might direct their efforts on the work they are supposed to be doing, or they may direct their efforts toward chatting with a coworker to get the latest office gossip. The intensity of one's efforts defines how strenuously one is going to push oneself toward a goal. Are they going to give it all they have and put their blood, sweat, and tears into the task, or are they going to give it only 50% effort? Lastly, motivation determines the persistence of one's efforts. When people feel truly motivated, they persist by staying on task until they reach a stopping point or a milestone, or they keep going until they finish the task or project. (Think about a time when you were working on a hobby or playing a video game and you needed "just two more minutes" to get to a stopping point. That's what genuine persistence feels like.) When there is little to no motivation, the direction of effort is not aimed squarely at the goal, the intensity of effort is not dialed to 100, and/or the persistence of effort fizzles well before reaching a milestone or the finish line.

Take Cersei as an example. Being married to King Robert Baratheon, she serves as Queen of Westeros. After Robert's death, Cersei does everything she can to retain control of the Iron Throne. This can be seen when we view and consider her actions and decisions. Think about the direction of her efforts, the intensity of her efforts, and the persistence of her efforts in pursing her goal. There is nothing she wouldn't (and doesn't) say or do in terms of her efforts toward reaching her goal of maintaining her grip on the Iron Throne. In other words, she is extremely extrinsically motivated to remain in power.

Expectancy Theory

Two theories that can help explain motivation are expectancy theory and goal-setting theory. Expectancy theory (Vroom, 1964) proposes that employees are motivated to perform when they believe they can successfully accomplish a task *and* when the rewards are worth the effort put in to accomplish that task. This theory suggests that motivation is a product of expectancy, instrumentality, and valence (or expectancy × instrumentality × valence). First, expectancy is defined as the belief that an exertion of effort will lead to some elevated level of performance. For instance, athletes would not put in the effort to train hard, eat right, and engage in practice sessions if they did not believe their efforts would result in an increased level of performance (running faster, jumping higher, throwing farther, etc.).

Next, instrumentality is defined as the belief that one's performance can and will lead to some desired outcome. If athletes do not believe that their performance of running faster, jumping higher, or throwing the ball farther would lead to their desired outcome of winning the match or the game, then they would not perform at an elevated level. Thus, instrumentality is important because it links the performance directly with a desired outcome.

Finally, the last element of expectancy theory is valence, which is the perceived or actual value of the outcome. Valence is important because if an outcome has little or no value (either perceived or actual value) to the employee, then there would be no reason to perform at a certain elevated level. For instance, an athlete trying out for the Olympics likely places a great deal of value on the outcome (a spot on the team). However, if the athlete is just performing the sport for fun (say, for a community fundraiser), their level of performance is probably not as heightened as during an Olympic tryout. To reiterate, expectancy theory argues that one's motivation is the product of expectancy, instrumentality, and valence. If any of these three elements is missing, then motivation would likely diminish or disappear altogether.

Continuing with the example of Cersei, we can apply the elements of expectancy theory to better understand why she is so motivated to keep her place on the throne. She demonstrates expectancy, that her exertion of effort will lead to enhanced performance. She believes that the harder she pushes herself, the better (i.e., more effective) her performance (i.e., her actions and behaviors) will be. Instrumentality is also present; she believes that her performance (i.e., her actions and decisions) will get her to her goal of keeping her seated on the Iron Throne. Lastly, the Iron Thorne, along with everything it represents and comes with (e.g., power, stature, wealth), is of extreme value to Cersei. In this way, expectancy theory can be used to help explain Cersei's motivation. She puts in effort to perform at a high level, because she believes her elevated level of performance will help her achieve her goal of remaining Queen of Westeros.

Goal-setting Theory

Similar to expectancy theory is goal-setting theory (Locke & Latham, 1990, 2002), which proposes that specific and high (or hard) goals result in a more elevated level of performance than easy, vague, and/or abstract goals (Locke & Latham, 2006). To clarify, goals are future outcomes people want or strive to achieve. In other words, they are the objectives for the actions people take. Goals must be both specific and difficult because specificity gives people a way to measure their progress toward achieving the goal, while difficulty pushes them to perform to the best of their ability.

Put simply, goal-setting theory states that goals lead to performance. However, the more nuanced and complex story is that there are mechanisms through which goals lead to performance, and this process is influenced by several factors. First, there are mechanisms that can impact the relationship between goals and performance, such as personality traits, level of autonomy, participation in decision-making processes, and incentives (Locke & Latham, 2006). Because these attributes differ from one circumstance to the next, and from one person to the other, individual and collective levels of motivation to achieve a goal can wax and wane. Then, there are four key factors that influence the goal-performance relationship. Locke and Latham (2006) identified these factors as feedback, which helps people track their progress; commitment to achieving the goal, which is enhanced when people believe they are capable of achieving the goal and when the goal is personally valuable; task complexity, because a goal that is too easy to complete is not stimulating; and situational constraints, such as having the right resources available and having any obstacles removed.

We could easily explore and explain many characters' motivation for seeking the Iron Throne using goal-setting theory: Stannis Baratheon, Daenerys Targaryen, Cersei Lannister, the list goes on. However, let's apply goal-setting theory to a more minor character with a simpler goal. Oberyn Martell of Dorne is driven by his goal to kill Gregor Clegane, also known as The Mountain, because Gregor violated and killed Oberyn's sister years earlier. Thus, Oberyn is motivated by his goal of getting revenge for his sister's death by killing Gregor. He sails all the way from Dorne to King's Landing for the chance to face Gregor, he arranges with Tyrion Lannister to fight Gregor in his place during Tyrion's trial by combat for the murder of King Joffrey Baratheon, and he makes a spectacle of his opportunity to achieve his goal. In terms of mechanisms between Oberyn's goal and his performance, there are many that keep him motivated, such as his high level of autonomy, because he is in complete control of his own thoughts and behaviors, and his incentive for achieving his goal, which is experiencing fulfillment and satisfaction for personally getting revenge for his sister's death.

Next, the four key factors are present and prominent, all of which bolster the relationship between performance and goal attainment. The first is feedback. Every time Oberyn deals a blow to Gregor, there is immediate feedback, such as Gregor's visible injuries and his audible groans, which let Oberyn know he is getting increasingly closer to his goal. The next is commitment; as Oberyn gets more closer to his goal, his commitment to his goal becomes much stronger because he can start to see Gregor's demise more concretely. At the beginning of the fight, Oberyn knows his goal, but he might not have been completely certain that he could achieve it. However, as the fight progresses and Gregor becomes progressively weaker, Oberyn's commitment to attaining his goal grows increasingly stronger. Then, task complexity fuels Oberyn's motivation. If killing Gregor were easy, the goal would likely not have been nearly as personally satisfying for Oberyn, and his motivation to put in his full effort to kill Gregor would likely not have been as robust. Lastly, situational constraints, such as Gregor's size and strength, impact the relationship between Oberyn's performance and his goal attainment. Ultimately, because of Gregor's size and strength, he manages to get up from what would have been a fatal blow for a normal-sized man and kills Oberyn, which, in the end, keeps Oberyn from achieving his goal.

Lastly, research has found that a variety of different goals can impact motivation, such as learning goals (as opposed to end goals; Seijts & Latham, 2001), group goals (as opposed to personal goals; DeShon et al., 2004; Seijts & Latham, 2000), and organization-level goals (as opposed to individual goals; Baum & Locke, 2004). Similarly, the way goals are framed (Drach-Zahavy & Erez, 2002) or subconsciously primed (Bargh & Williams, 2006; Stajkovic et al., 2006) can also impact people's motivation to perform in order to achieve goals. Often, when we know, for example, that our team is counting on us to do well, we are more motivated to perform than if we think nobody is looking.

As demonstrated by many of the characters in *Game of Thrones*, motivation is a strong force that can help in accomplishing many tasks and, if used correctly, achieving goals. In our own organizations, managers and leaders who want to achieve organizational goals must find ways to provide their workers with both intrinsic and extrinsic motivation. While monetary bonuses are generally well received by employees, it is not realistic to always offer financial incentives. Effective leaders should and do find ways to also develop intrinsic motivation in their employees, such as designing and assigning tasks that offer employees the opportunity to develop new skills, setting difficult but realistic and achievable goals, offering flexibility (e.g., work schedules, working from home), allowing teams to define their own goals (within certain parameters), or even framing organizational goals so that they appeal to employees on a personal level. Offering these types of incentives can often lead to intrinsic motivation because of people's desire to reciprocate gestures (Blau, 1964).

Summary

We have defined motivation in this chapter, and explored what causes motivation and what some of its elements and determinants are. We discussed the following concepts about motivation:

- Motivation is made of the internal and external forces that cause people to want to put in effort to engage in goal-directed behaviors while also influencing the intensity and persistence of those actions and efforts.
- Expectancy theory proposes that expectancy, instrumentality, and valence must all be present for people to be motivated. Expectancy is the belief that more effort will equal more performance, instrumentality is the belief that better performance will lead to reaching the outcome, and valence is the belief that the outcome has either some perceived or real value.
- Goal-setting theory suggests that goals lead to performance when the goal is specific and difficult, but attainable. The way goals are framed can also impact how motivated people are likely to be in working toward achieving them.

We have discussed in this chapter the importance of motivation, explored what motivation looks like, and examined what it helped characters in *Game of Thrones* to achieve. We now turn our attention to trust, in large part because leaders cannot work to motivate their followers and employees if their followers and employees do not trust them.

Chapter 8

Trust

One of the foundational elements of any relationship is trust, which is defined as the extent of one's willingness to be vulnerable to another party (Mayer et al., 1995). The basis of trust is that behaviors and events will and do occur the way people expect, rather than in a manner they fear (Deutsch, 1973). Research has shown that trust is one of the criteria by which we assess our leaders (Bews & Rossouw, 2002) because if leaders are not deemed trustworthy by their followers, then they often lose credibility among them. In the workplace, we need to have trust in the people with whom we work, such as our subordinates, peers, and supervisors, if we hope to accomplish our personal and organizational goals. This is not unlike what the characters in *Game of Thrones* must do in order to achieve their goals, particularly the ones who hope to seize and sit on the Iron Throne: put their trust in others.

Why Trust Matters

One question that arises about trust in organization is why it matters. What's so important about trust in the workplace that makes it worth discussing? One answer to this question is that for organizations to function effectively, managers must trust their employees, with the reverse also being vital: employees must trust their managers. That is, there is an interdependence between managers and employees that is required in order for organizations to reach their goals (Mayer et al., 1995). As a foundational requirement in any relationship, trust allows one party to be confident that another party will do what is expected. This is crucial in organizations because it is not likely or realistic that organizational leaders and managers have unlimited time and resources to constantly monitor all their individual employees' behaviors, actions, and decisions at all times. Thus, they must take risks and leave themselves vulnerable to the decisions and actions of their employees. In other words, they must trust their employees to make decisions and enact behaviors that are in the best interest of the organization and that work toward achieving organizational goals. Similarly, employees don't always have the opportunity or authority to make decisions that directly impact themselves (for instance, many employees do not necessarily get to create their own work

Bend the Knee or Seize the Throne: Leadership Lessons from the Seven Kingdoms, 51–56
Copyright © 2023 by Nathan Tong and Michael J. Urick
Published under exclusive licence by Emerald Publishing Limited
doi:10.1108/978-1-80262-647-620231008

schedule, purchase or update the equipment they need, or determine the amount of their salary increase). So, they must take risks and leave themselves vulnerable to the decisions and actions of their managers. This means they must trust their managers and trust that their managers will make the best decisions for them.

In *Game of Thrones*, the development of trust, as well as the absence or abuse (betrayal) of trust, are some of the main elements that continually drive the story forward. Ned Stark trusted his friend Robert Baratheon and, by default, Robert's family, but he is ultimately beheaded by a Baratheon (i.e., Robert's son Joffrey). Catelyn and Robb Stark trusted Walder Frey as a friend and ally, and Walder trusted Robb and Catelyn to keep their promise of Robb marrying one of his daughters, but both Catelyn and Robb are killed because Robb does not fulfill his promise of marrying one of Walder's daughters. Sansa Stark trusted Petyr Baelish (Littlefinger) to lead her to safety after being used as a pawn after her father's death, but he abuses Sansa's trust (i.e., he betrays her trust) by marrying her off to Ramsay Bolton, who physically and mentally tortures her. There are numerous other instances of the characters in *Game of Thrones* putting their trust in others, some that end for the better and some that end for the worse.

In the series, there are also numerous examples of the absence of trust. For instance, because Daenerys Targaryen could understand what Kraznys mo Nakloz is saying (unbeknownst to him) as he speaks Valyrian during their negotiation of buying the Army of Unsullied, she knows she cannot trust him (more on this in a moment). As another example, Sansa and Arya Stark, separately, cannot find valid reasons to trust Brienne of Tarth to protect them. They have no idea that Brienne had promised Catelyn Stark (before her death) that she would protect them, but Sansa and Arya do not know this. Lastly, there are times when trust is abused. For example, toward the end of the series, Daenerys trusts those around her to keep her secret about who Jon Snow really is. However, her trust is betrayed by a number of people including Jon, Sansa, Tyrion Lannister, and Lord Varys. Ultimately, Varys pays for his abuse of Daenerys' trust with his life when he is set ablaze by one of Daenerys' dragons at her command.

Types of Trust

Research has suggested that trust can be based on one of three characteristics: disposition, cognition, and affect (McAllister, 1995; Robert et al., 2009). First, disposition-based trust refers to the trust that people naturally have toward others, or in other words, their tendency to be willing to depend on other people (McKnight et al., 1998). While some people are naturally and instinctively more trusting of people they don't know, others are inherently more skeptical. Disposition-based trust has little to do with the observed behaviors or perceived intentions of others. Instead, it concerns the focal person and how much (or how little) they generally trust other people. There are a host of factors that shape people's individual tendency to trust others, such as upbringing (Webb et al., 1986) and national culture (Johnson & Cullen, 2002). Scholars (e.g., Stack, 1978) have demonstrated that as children grow up, they tend to be more trusting of others when their needs are met and less trusting of others when they repeatedly experience disappointment. This tendency to generally trust (or not trust) others is continuously shaped by daily experiences, such as interactions with friends or at school (Stack, 1978).

In *Game of Thrones*, both Sansa and Arya Stark are young children at the beginning of the series. Being raised by Ned and Catelyn in a safe and loving home environment at Winterfell, both girls are initially (at the start of the series) naturally very trusting of others, even those whom they do not know. In other words, they had high levels of disposition-based trust. As the series unfolds, the girls' trust in others is repeatedly broken, teaching them that people cannot be trusted. Sansa learns this the hard way after numerous people break her trust. For example, Joffrey tells her that he would not kill her father, but then he does so anyway. Others who break her trust include Tywin Lannister, who forces her to marry Tyrion, and even her own aunt Lysa Arryn, who tries to murder Sansa.

Arya experiences multiple betrayals of trust herself as well, which diminishes her disposition-based trust. After watching her father get beheaded, she runs off on her own. Arya is unsure of whom she can trust after this happens because the same family that welcomed her family to King's Landing is the same family that beheads her father. In her travels, she runs into, and is taken captive by, Sandor Clegane, better known in the show as The Hound. She recognizes him as a guard who served Joffrey Lannister, causing her to not trust him. And because Sandor knows who Arya is and what she's worth as a Stark, he takes her captive with plans to ransom her to her aunt, Lysa Arryn.

Cognition-based trust, the second type of trust, stems from experiences with specific people and/or situations (Lewis & Wiegert, 1985; McAllister, 1995). After some number of interactions with another person, we begin to recognize that we can trust that person (or not trust them). Scholars have explained that with cognition-based trust, "we choose whom we will trust in which respects and under what circumstances, and we base the choice on what we take to be 'good reasons'" (Lewis & Wiegert, 1985, p. 970). As an example, you may not immediately trust your new manager at work, no matter whether you are new or they are new. Although they are your new manager, you might by unsure about what type of person they are. For example, will they take credit for your ideas? Will they advocate for you every time the opportunity to do so presents itself? And will they have your best interest in mind when making decisions? After working with them for a while, you will begin to recognize the "good reasons" why you can (or cannot) trust your manager based on your interactions and experiences with them.

Researchers have suggested that cognition-based trust is primarily an assessment of a leader's (and others') trustworthiness, and this trustworthiness is evaluated on three dimensions: ability, benevolence, and integrity (Colquitt & Rodell, 2011; Mayer et al., 1995). Ability refers to the extent to which a leader has the capacity and facility to complete specific tasks with competence, skill, and efficiency. Benevolence refers to the belief that a leader has the employees' best interest in mind, as opposed to operating based on selfish motives that benefit the leader themself rather than the group or the organization. Lastly, integrity refers to the belief that a leader behaves based on sound values and principles accepted and/or shared by the group.

Mayer et al. (1995) argued that trustworthiness is not an either/or proposition. That is, leaders are not simply seen as either trustworthy or untrustworthy. Instead, trustworthiness is assessed on a continuum, with one end being completely trustworthy and the other end being completely untrustworthy. Similarly, the three dimensions of cognition-based trust (ability, benevolence, and integrity) can also vary independently along a continuum. For instance, a leader might have high levels of ability, but low levels of benevolence and integrity. In a situation like this, employees might trust the leader in certain areas, like getting tasks completed because of their ability, but may not generally trust the leader overall because although the leader is ranked highly in ability, they also have low levels of benevolence and integrity.

Cognition-based trust is demonstrated throughout Daenerys Targaryen's story arc in the series. Early in the show, she trusts her brother Viserys to protect her while he seeks to take back the Iron Throne. However, she quickly learns that he will do whatever it takes to become King of Westeros, including, in his own words, letting all the Dothraki men (who number in the thousands) have their way with her. His behaviors demonstrate to Daenerys that she cannot trust him because he does not have benevolence or integrity. Later in the series, she interacts with Kraznys mo Nakloz, a slave trader and one of the Good Masters of Astapor, to buy Unsullied soldiers. Working through Missandei as an interpreter, Daenerys learns that she cannot trust Kraznys because of the words he uses when he speaks. Kraznys only speaks Low Valyrian and not the Common Tongue, so he is unable to communicate directly with Daenerys (or so he thinks). What he does not realize is that Daenerys understands Valyrian, and she has been listening to his exact words rather than just to Missandei's translations, which she edits to be more diplomatic. Based on Daenerys' interactions with Kraznys, she finds what he actually says is not in line with what he has Missandei translate. In this way, he does not show benevolence or integrity, demonstrating to Daenerys some "good reasons" why she cannot trust him.

Finally, affect-based trust is based on the emotional bonds people have with others (Lewis & Wiegert, 1985). When we form emotional bonds with others that go beyond just the interactions we have with them, we become invested in those relationships such that we genuinely care for those people and believe that our feelings will be reciprocated (Pennings & Woiceshyn, 1987). These emotional bonds form the foundation for affect-based trust. Using our previous workplace example, we might trust our manager based on our interactions with them. However, the trust we have in our managers at our workplaces likely do not raise the level of affect-based trust because we do not usually form an emotional bond with our managers the same way we form emotional bonds with, for example, our significant other or our friends.

One of the most notable examples of affect-based trust in *Game of Thrones* is the trust between Tyrion Lannister and Shae. Although Shae is initially hired as a prostitute for Tyrion, the two of them develop feelings for one another. Throughout the show, she demonstrates through her actions that she trusts Tyrion to do what is best for the two of them. For example, before the Battle of the Blackwater,

Tyrion tells Shae that she should leave for her own safety, but she defies his request and stays with him because she trusts him to keep her safe. Ultimately, they betray each other's trust. First, after being forced by his father Tywin to marry Sansa, Tyrion calls Shae a whore to her face before believing he sends her away on a ship. In retaliation for Tyrion breaking her trust (and her heart), Shae then betrays Tyrion's trust by testifying against him at his trial for Joffrey's murder. The trust that existed between these characters, before it was lost, was based on the emotional bond between them. The trust between them hinged on how they felt about each other rather than on a rational assessment of each other's track record of demonstrated behaviors.

Outcomes of Trust

Once trust is established between people, both parties are changed. In their research, Mayer et al. (1995) explained that there is a marked difference between trusting someone and exhibiting trust toward someone. When an employee trusts a leader, there is a *willingness* to assume some risk and be vulnerable to that leader. However, exhibiting trust entails *actually* assuming risk and making oneself vulnerable. After trust is built between people, there should be not just a *feeling* of trust between them, but a *demonstration* of trust via visible or tangible risk-taking behaviors.

The difference between having trust and exhibiting trust can be seen throughout *Game of Thrones*. One example is the trust between Ramsay Bolton and Theon Greyjoy. After being captured and tortured at Dreadfort, Theon believes he is freed by Ramsay. As Theon flees to Deepwood Motte, he is attacked by several men. However, Ramsey saves Theon from the attackers and leads him to what he believes is safety. However, to Theon's horror, Ramsay brings him back to Dreadfort and continues to torture him. After believing Ramsay freed him and subsequently "saved" him, Theon initially feels trust toward Ramsay. That is, he has a willingness to assume risk and be vulnerable to Ramsay based on "good reasons." However, when he (blindly) follows Ramsay to what he believes is safety, that is when Theon actually assumes risk and makes himself vulnerable. Unfortunately, Theon's trust in Ramsay is misplaced, and Ramsay ultimately betrays Theon's trust by continuing to torture him.

The tables are later turned when Ramsay has to exhibit trust in Theon, who at that point is known as Reek. As Ramsay attempts to take Moat Cailin, he needs Reek's help. He can take Moat Cailin more easily if Reek, posing as Theon Greyjoy, can get the Ironborn men who are holding Moat Cailin to allow Ramsay and his men safe passage. Ramsay takes a risk and leaves himself vulnerable to Reek because he does not know for sure whether Reek will reclaim his identity as Theon once he is in the safety of the Ironborn stronghold. If he does, then Ramsay will have lost both Reek and the opportunity to take Moat Cailin. Ramsay has to take a risk and trust Reek, which leaves him vulnerable to Reek's actions. Fortunately for Ramsay, his trust is not misplaced because Reek ends up doing exactly what is asked of him.

When Trust Matters

So far, we've talked about why trust matters, what types of trust exist, and what their bases and outcomes are. But is trust equally important across all types of situations? Research suggests the answer is no. In a series of studies, Brockner et al. (1997) found that employees' trust in organizational leaders typically leads to supporting those leaders (and the organization) when concerns about trust are highlighted because of unfavorable outcomes (Brockner et al., 1997), unexpected outcomes (Pyszczynski & Greenberg, 1981; Wong & Weiner, 1981), or both. During these incidents, people engage in sensemaking behaviors (Weick, 1995) to try to determine who or what should be blamed or credited for what happened since the result is not what they expected and/or does not benefit them. Thus, there are circumstances and contexts when trust is more likely, or less likely, to impact how people react to the decisions their leaders make.

Summary

This chapter has explored the importance of trust and explained how trust is demonstrated between numerous different characters in *Game of Thrones*. The use (and abuse) of trust is largely what drives the plot of the series forward. After analyzing these instances of trust, leaders should remember:

- Trust is essential between parties in any relationship, and this includes in the workplace. At some point, each person in an organization will be vulnerable to someone else, regardless of position or hierarchy.
- In organizations, employees will be vulnerable to the decisions and actions of their managers, but at the same time, managers are also vulnerable to the decisions and actions of their employees.
- In the workplace, managers should take steps to build cognition-based trust with and among their employees by demonstrating ability, benevolence, and integrity.

One of the major aspects of trust that employees can have in their supervisor is their supervisor will treat them fairly. In other words, employees often trust that their supervisor will show justice in their words and actions. Feeling fairly treated at work is important to people, and it can often be taken for granted until unfair treatment happens. So, we explore justice in our next chapter.

Chapter 9

Justice

It goes without saying that in the workplace, managers and organizational leaders strive to employ workers who are happy, motivated, and productive. One simple way to achieve this goal is to treat people fairly, which can be achieved no matter whether a leader is bending the knee or seizing the throne. This is something many of the characters in *Game of Thrones*, such as Sansa Stark, Daenerys Targaryen, Lord Varys, and Jon Snow, understand all too well. But what is the connection between fair treatment and happy, motivated employees? How do people evaluate fair treatment at work? And what happens if people feel unfairly treated? In this chapter, we will discuss why justice matters, explore how employees assess justice and determine what is fair or unfair, and examine what happens when people feel like they are treated unfairly.

Identification and a Sense of Belonging

In general, people like to feel valued because it makes them feel like they are an important part of the group(s) they belong to. Social identity theory (Tajfel & Turner, 1979, 2004) suggests that people see themselves as part of a social group or groups (e.g., political parties, religious organizations, sports teams, sports leagues, workgroups, etc.), and their affiliation with those groups provides them with not only a sense of belonging but also with a sense of self-definition (Hogg et al., 1995) and identification (Kreiner & Ashforth, 2004). Employees in organizations want to feel like they are an important part of a group, and there are many different groups at work that employees can identify with, such as their immediate workgroup, their department, their location, or even the organization as a whole.

In *Game of Thrones*, there are also many different groups that the characters can and do belong to that provide them with a sense of identity. The most obvious of these are the houses, such as House Lannister, House Stark, House Tyrell, and House Greyjoy, but there are also groups that are not houses, such as the Wildlings (who call themselves the Free Folk), the Night's Watch, the White Walkers, and the Dothraki. Each of these groups has its own distinct characteristics and its own identity, which give its group members a sense of not only who they are, but also a sense of self-worth and feeling valued for being part of that group.

Bend the Knee or Seize the Throne: Leadership Lessons from the Seven Kingdoms, 57–65
Copyright © 2023 by Nathan Tong and Michael J. Urick
Published under exclusive licence by Emerald Publishing Limited
doi:10.1108/978-1-80262-647-620231009

One example of an affiliation leading to a strong sense of identity is Mance Rayder. As the leader of the Free Folk, he so strongly identifies as one of the Free Folk that he refuses to bend the knee to anyone, which is one of the core values of the Free Folk. Even when he faces being burned alive, he refuses to bend the knee to Stannis Baratheon. Doing so would have meant that he could stay alive and help keep the other Free Folk safe. However, his strong identification as one of the Free Folk means he must refuse to bend the knee, and he is burned alive as a result (although Jon Snow kills him with an arrow to heart so that he does not suffer).

Why Justice is Important

One way in which managers and organizational leaders can promote perceptions of belonging and feeling valued among their employees is by treating them fairly. Fair treatment toward employees promotes a sense of justice and belonging in organizations, and has been shown to bolster employees' motivation, sense of self-worth, engagement in prosocial behaviors, and other similar positive attitudes and behaviors (Hoffman et al., 2007; Organ, 1988). This can be explained in large part by social exchange theory (Blau, 1964), which proposes that there is an unspoken social norm that people feel they should receive back a fair return on their investments in social exchanges. In other words, social exchange theory proposes that people invest themselves (e.g., their time, energy, and attention) in others because they expect that the other party will return the gesture, either immediately or in the future. In order to maintain a sense of balance between what people give and what they receive, people have a strong tendency to "return the favor." That is, if people feel they have been treated fairly, then they will do something positive in return to reciprocate the positivity (i.e., the fair treatment) that was given to them.

This type of behavior can be seen many times in *Game of Thrones*. For example, those who perceive themselves as being a part of or loyal to a house or a group will exhibit positive attitudes and behaviors toward that house or group when the leader (or leaders) of that house or group treat them fairly. Throughout the series, Daenerys does her best to be a fair leader. Her decisions and actions in nearly every situation are guided by what she believes are the most fair and correct thing to do. Because she behaves this way, her followers are loyal to her and behave in ways that help her and benefit her in her pursuit of the Iron Throne. Whether it is with her direct personal advisers like Ser Jorah Mormont, Missandei, Grey Worm, or with one of the thousands of people she helps to free from slavery, Daenerys treats people fairly and, in return, they engage in prosocial behaviors that benefit her, her quest for the Iron Throne, and/or each other as a community. For instance, when Daenerys first interacts with Missandei and Grey Worm, she treats them like human beings with thoughts, feelings, desires, and ambitions, whereas Kraznys mo Nakloz treated them like slaves who were worth nothing more than the actions they could perform to benefit him. (We will discuss more specifics about the outcomes of fair treatment below.) While fair treatment used in conjunction with transactional leadership can benefit leaders and organizations, treating people fairly can be used even more effectively with transformational leadership (see Chapter 2 on leadership styles).

Unsurprisingly and unfortunately, the opposite of fair treatment is also true: when people feel unfairly treated, their perceptions of injustice lead to a host of negative attitudes and behaviors such as sabotage, incivility, withdrawal, and, in a worst-case scenario for organizations, turnover (Fox et al., 2001). There are many instances in the series when people feel they have been treated unfairly, but perhaps the strongest demonstration of injustice in *Game of Thrones* happens when King Joffrey Baratheon makes the decision to execute Ned Stark, and then carries out his decision. In the following section, we will examine the four dimensions of justice individually, and explore why, as a leader, Joffrey's decisions and actions leading to Ned Stark's beheading are particularly unfair.

Four Dimensions of Justice

Research has demonstrated that perceptions of justice can be evaluated along four dimensions: distributive justice, procedural justice, interpersonal justice, and informational justice (Colquitt, 2001). In a nutshell, distributive justice considers the fairness of the outcomes people receive, procedural justice examines the fairness of the process(es) used to reach those outcomes, interpersonal justice assesses the fairness of treatment from others, and informational justice evaluates the fairness of information and explanations provided (Colquitt, 2001). Let's work our way through Ned's demise at the hands of Joffrey using these four dimensions one at a time to better understand why Joffrey's actions are unfair.

The first dimension of justice is distributive justice, which primarily considers the outcome of a leader's decisions or actions relative to an employee's perceptions of their input. The important question with distributive justice is: do the results or rewards received (i.e., the outcomes) match the effort that was put in, or, as the saying goes, does the punishment fit the crime? In the case of Joffrey executing Ned, distributive justice looks at the outcome based on Ned's input, or what Ned did or didn't do. That is, does the outcome Ned receives (death by beheading) match the behaviors he exhibited (threatening to expose Cersei's secret)? Without getting too philosophical about the ethical considerations of an execution (see Chapter 6 for a discussion on ethics), Joffrey's execution of Ned is largely seen as unfair because the outcome is not fitting in relation to Ned's actions. From most people's perspective, Ned has not done anything wrong that would warrant his death; he simply wants to speak the truth. Thus, his beheading seems unfair, at least based on distributive justice, because the level and severity of the outcome he receives does not correspond to the level or severity of his actions.

The second justice dimension is procedural justice, which considers the fairness of the process(es) used to reach an outcome, such as, in organizations, distributing or allocating resources (e.g., time, money, materials, promotions) to decide who gets what. Rather than considering whether the outcomes match the inputs like distributive justice does, procedural justice looks at the fairness of the process(es) used to arrive at a specific outcome. When an outcome initially seems unfair, people tend to turn their attention to the processes used to arrive at that outcome (Lind & Tyler, 1988) to assess whether the outcome should be seen as fair (or unfair). This is because when an outcome seems unfair but the process to get to that outcome was fair, then the outcome should also be deemed fair (Greenberg & Tyler, 1987).

There are six rules associated with procedural justice: accuracy, bias suppression, consistency, correctability, representativeness, and voice (Colquitt et al., 2001; Folger, 1977; Leventhal, 1980; Lind et al., 1990). Accuracy represents the extent to which decisions are made based on accurate information. Bias suppression is the extent to which favoritism or dislike are minimized when making decisions. Consistency reflects the extent to which rules and policies are applied in the same way across time, people, situations, and/or contexts. Correctability denotes the extent to which an outcome can be rectified or changed if an outcome is in fact unfair. Representativeness refers to the extent to which the people who will be impacted by a decision are allowed to be involved in the decision-making process. And lastly, voice represents the extent to which employees have a say in decision-making processes.

The rules of accuracy, consistency, bias suppression, and representativeness are meant to ensure that the rules and procedures used to make decisions are objective and neutral so as not to favor or privilege, or disadvantage, any one person or group. The rules of correctability and voice afford people the opportunity to influence or appeal a decision if the application of a rule or policy seems biased or unfair.

For an action or decision to be seen as fair, the rules of procedural justice must exist during the decision-making process. Unfortunately for Ned Stark, none of these rules are present when Joffrey decides to execute him. Ned has no say in the matter, and those who advocate for his life could not convince Joffrey to change his mind about his decision to execute Ned. Joffrey's decision is not based on accurate information about Ned, he does not suppress his bias against Ned, the execution is not consistent with any punishment (or inaction) others in Ned's position typically receive, the action is not correctable, and Ned receives neither representativeness nor voice as or after Joffrey makes his decision. Thus, based on the rules of procedural justice, most people would likely argue that Ned is not treated fairly.

Interpersonal justice centers on how fairly someone feels they are treated by another person (e.g., a supervisor or a leader). Generally, interpersonal treatment is seen as being fair when the treatment from that other person exhibits dignity, respect, and politeness (Colquitt, 2001; Holtz & Harold, 2013). In the show, Joffrey shows little to no interpersonal justice toward Ned because what little direct interaction he has with Ned demonstrates no dignity, no respect, and no politeness. Joffrey forces Ned to confess that he tried to seize the Iron Throne by attempting to kill him after Robert Baratheon's death. The way Joffrey carries out the execution publicly, after Ned publicly confesses to treasonous actions he didn't engage in, is precisely the opposite of treating Ned with dignity, respect, and politeness. Joffrey could have carried out the execution in private after the confession to give Ned some dignity, but one of Joffrey's goals is to demonstrate his power as the king to the people of Westeros by publicly executing Ned. And in doing so, he does not show Ned any interpersonal justice.

Lastly, informational justice occurs when people feel they have been given truthful and adequate explanations in an honest and candid manner (Colquitt, 2001; Patient & Skarlicki, 2010). Although interpersonal and informational justice used to be thought of together under the concept of interactional justice (Bies & Moag, 1986), more recent research has shown them to be distinct perceptions (Colquitt, 2001). This difference can be seen in the show in the way Joffrey treats Ned and carries out his execution. We just discussed that Joffrey shows Ned no interpersonal justice because his treatment toward Ned showed no dignity, respect, or politeness. This can be contrasted with what Joffrey says to Ned, that is, the information Ned is given from Joffrey. In other words, the way Joffrey treats Ned is distinct from the information he gives to Ned. Joffrey tells Ned that if he confesses to engaging in treason by trying to kill him, his life would be spared. Joffrey even tells this to Sansa, in an effort to convince her to get her father (Ned) to confess to treason. However, after Ned's public confession, Joffrey orders Ned's execution immediately. This violates the rule of informational justice because Joffrey did not provide Ned, or Sansa, with truthful or adequate information in an honest and candid manner. In fact, the exact opposite happens; Joffrey says one thing and then does the complete opposite, which directly violates the rule of informational justice. Thus, Joffrey's actions do not demonstrate informational justice.

Overall Justice

More recently, research has revealed that although people can distinguish between the four types of justice, they primarily consider how fairly they feel treated at work (e.g., by their supervisor) based on overall justice (Ambrose & Schminke, 2009). Overall justice proposes that instead of considering each dimension of justice individually and distinctly when thinking about how fairly they feel treated, people evaluate fairness in a more holistic manner (Ambrose & Schminke, 2009; Greenberg, 2001). Scholars have shown that perceptions of overall justice help to explain the relationship between the individual dimensions of justice and the resulting attitudes and behaviors associated with fair (and unfair) treatment (Ambrose & Schminke, 2009).

Using the example above, someone in Ned's position likely doesn't think about the fairness of the outcome, the decision-making process, the personal treatment, and/or the information as separate and individual pieces. As scholars have shown (e.g., Ambrose & Schminke, 2009), people can identify and evaluate these dimensions of justice when asked to do so, but in general, when assessing how fairly they feel treated, people tend to evaluate the overall situation and their general treatment rather than reflecting on separate parts and pieces. In Ned's case, the situation is likely perceived by most people to be unfair because most people consider and evaluate the overall situation and associated outcomes rather than considering each dimension of justice separately.

So, organizational supervisors and managers should work to ensure that their employees feel that they are treated fairly in general. Minor infractions of individual justice dimensions (such as an inconsequential outcome that seems unfair) probably will not elicit a strong negative reaction (and retaliation) from employees so long as they generally feel they are treated fairly overall.

Outcomes of Justice

As mentioned earlier, research has shown that, when people perceive that they are being treated fairly at work they engage in prosocial behaviors that benefit other individuals in the workplace, as well as positive behaviors that benefit the organization (Organ, 1988). Scholars have named these actions organizational citizenship behaviors. Similarly, when people feel unfairly treated, they tend to engage in harmful behaviors that negatively affect the work environment, the people in the work environment (e.g., peers, supervisors, customers; Masterson, 2001), and/or the organization itself. These actions have been termed counterproductive workplace behaviors (e.g., Martinko et al., 2002). In the next sections, we will explore each of these types of behaviors.

Organizational Citizenship Behaviors

Organizational Citizenship Behaviors (OCBs) are those actions employees perform that fall outside of and/or go beyond their work duties and responsibilities that make a positive impact on the workplace. OCBs were defined by researcher Dennis Organ (1988) as "individual behavior that is discretionary, not directly or explicitly recognized by the [organization's] formal reward system, and that in the aggregate promotes the effective functioning of the organization" (p. 4).

According to Organ (1988, 1990), OCBs include altruism, cheerleading, courtesy, conscientiousness, civic virtue, peacekeeping, and sportsmanship. Later research showed that managers have difficulty distinguishing between altruism, courtesy, peacekeeping, and cheerleading, as they all appear to be helping behaviors, which are actions that assist others with their work-related tasks and duties or otherwise prevent problems from happening at work (Podsakoff et al., 1997). As an example of this type of OCB, an employee might pick up a random piece of trash they see in the hallway and put it in the garbage can. This is not part of the employee's job (unless they are a member of the maintenance crew) and they might not necessarily be recognized or rewarded for their action, but it makes for a better work environment for everyone.

Of the other remaining OCBs, civic virtue is characterized by employee behaviors that demonstrate a genuine concern about the organization's well-being, conscientiousness is defined as employees' willingness to accept and follow organizational rules and policies, and sportsmanship is identified as employees' willingness to weather their work conditions, no matter how bad they might get, without complaining (Organ, 1988). As you can probably see, regardless of what or how OCBs are named or labeled, they are those behaviors employees engage in that positively benefit the organization and/or its employees but are not formally recognized or rewarded for being done.

In *Game of Thrones*, Grey Worm engages in many behaviors throughout the series that would be considered OCBs, if we think of Daenerys and her all followers as an organization, with Daenerys as the leader in charge. As we discussed above, Daenerys almost always treats all her followers, which includes Grey Worm, as fairly as possible. In response to this fair treatment, Grey Worm often goes beyond his call of duty to keep things peaceful, improve their "organization," and help others. An example of one of his OCBs is when Daenerys hosts the captains of the Second Sons, Mero of Braavos and Prendahl na Ghezen, and their lieutenant, Daario Naharis. During their discussion to try to forge an alliance, Mero behaves extremely offensively, saying vulgar things to and about Daenerys and acting crudely toward Missandei. Grey Worm sees this insulting behavior and verbally volunteers to cut out Mero's tongue for Daenerys, which she declines. Certainly, as Daenerys' guard, Grey Worm's job is to protect her. However, in this particular situation, she does not ask for or need Grey Worm's help, and that is precisely what makes Grey Worm's actions in this scene an OCB. He engages in a behavior that goes beyond what is required of his work tasks to help improve the overall "work" environment. And he engages in this OCB in large part because Daenerys consistently treats him fairly.

Counterproductive Workplace Behaviors

As we mentioned above, and as you might expect, when people feel like they are treated unfairly in the workplace, they engage in retaliatory behaviors that negatively impact the work environment, other people (such as employees and customers), and/or the organization as a whole. In the same way that fair treatment signals that someone is a valued and important member of a group, injustice or unfair treatment is often viewed as an indication that one is inconsequential to the group, that one does not matter. This is in line with social exchange theory (Blau, 1964) in that just as positive treatment is expected to be reciprocated, negative treatment is oftentimes reciprocated as well.

These negative behaviors are referred to as Counterproductive Workplace Behaviors (CWBs). In general, CWBs are defined as deviant behaviors that blatantly disregard organizational values and/or violate organizational policies (Collins & Griffin, 1998; Hogan & Hogan, 1989). These behaviors can range in significance and seriousness from low (such as chronic tardiness and absenteeism) to high (such as theft, assault, violence, and turnover). They can also vary in terms of the intended target, ranging from harmful to one or a few people (such as gossip and incivility toward others, or intentionally poor customer service) to harming the organization (such as sabotage, intentionally wasting company resources, or slandering the company's reputation). CWBs can take many forms, but what they all have in common is that they are harmful to the organization and/or its people (employees, customers, and other stakeholders).

Continuing our example of Joffrey from above, he exhibits many instances of unfair treatment. Aside from beheading Ned Stark, there is also the time when he makes a group of dwarves reenact the War of the Five Kings during his wedding to Margery Tyrell. Nobody at the wedding finds the reenactment amusing. In fact, the wedding guests are all visibly and audibly disgusted by it, but Joffrey laughs hysterically and shows complete disregard for the revulsion his wedding guests are displaying. If he had wanted to treat his guests fairly, he would have stopped the show immediately when they found it distasteful and showed their disdain. In addition to this, he also mocks Tyrion Lannister by suggesting that he take one of the performer's costumes and join in the reenactment. (Joffrey's behavior in this entire scene would be in line with violation of interpersonal justice: not treating others with dignity and respect.) Understanding that Joffrey treats people unfairly, we can see many characters engage in CWBs in retaliation to the way Joffrey treats them. Some of them plot against Joffrey because of the injustice he shows to people. But one of the immediate CWB responses we see after the reenactment is Tyrion pouring a cup of wine on Joffrey's head. This is a CWB in that it violates both the values and the rules of the kingdom because the king should always be treated with the utmost respect. Then, Olenna Tyrell's action of poisoning Joffrey is also a CWB, perhaps the most serious one in the show, because it results in Joffrey's death. (Certainly, there are many reasons why Olenna wants Joffrey dead, but his unfair treatment of others is one of these reasons.) As these behaviors demonstrate, when people feel like they are or have been treated unfairly, especially by a leader, they will engage in behaviors that are harmful for the workplace, its people, and/or the organization itself.

Having examined and discussed the outcomes of both fair and unfair treatment, it is obvious that organizational managers and leaders would be wise to do their best to make sure their employees feel fairly treated at work in order to get the most optimal performance from them. Perceptions of fair treatment make people feel like they matter and typically result in engagement in OCBs, while perceptions of being treated unfairly often lead to harmful consequences in the form of CWBs.

Summary

This chapter has explored why fairness matters to employees, and ways in which they evaluate how fairly they feel they have been treated.

- Justice and fair treatment matter because they make people feel like a valued member of the group(s) they see themselves belonging to and provide them with their identity.
- Justice can be assessed along four dimensions: distributive justice, procedural justice, interpersonal justice, and informational justice.
- Although people can recognize and assess each of the four justice dimensions, they primarily evaluate the fairness of a situation or event based on their perceptions of overall justice.
- Perceived fair treatment activates a host of positive behaviors, called OCBs, that can benefit organizational members, the workplace environment, and/or the organization itself.
- Perceived unfair treatment can lead to negative behaviors, called CWBs, that can cause harm to organizational stakeholders, the work environment, and/or the organization.

Organizational leaders and managers have many opportunities to demonstrate and exhibit fair treatment to others. They can show fairness in their day-to-day interactions with others, such as employees, buyers, and suppliers. There are also instances of robust interactions with others when fair treatment can be displayed. One of these times is during negotiations, which is the focus of our next chapter.

Chapter 10

Negotiation

Scholars (e.g., Fairhurst & Connaughton, 2014) have proposed that communication defines, constitutes, and is central to leadership. In other words, communication is what makes leadership, leadership. (See Chapter 4 for a more robust exploration of communication.) Additionally, one of the important functions of communication is negotiation—a process during which people engage in discussions to exchange one or more items or services of value for another (Pruitt, 1971; Short, 1974). For example, in organizations, people negotiate over resources such as salaries, material costs, work schedules, and even bonuses and rewards. If the primary aim of leadership is to get others to take action toward accomplishing a common goal, then one effective way to achieve this goal is through negotiation. Without negotiation, it would be difficult to imagine people who work together accomplishing anything significant or meaningful because, according to agency theory (Eisenhardt, 1989), individuals typically act in their own best interest, as opposed to the best interest of the group or organization.

What Negotiation is (and is Not)

For many people, the idea of negotiation is perceived as a fight, an argument, or a conflict in which two or more parties are struggling to get or maintain power by "battling" over who gets "more" of some desired outcome. However, negotiation is not, and should not be seen as, a fight or a battle. Instead, negotiation is, and should be perceived as, a process in which two or more parties come together to find a mutually beneficial agreement or arrangement (Pruitt, 1971) in which all parties are better off than they were prior to the negotiation.

Certainly, there are times when a negotiation is over a finite or limited set of resources. This can be thought of as a negotiation over fixed amount of "pie" in which the amount that one party gains, the other party necessarily loses. For example, if one party gets 70% of a pie, that means there is a maximum of 30% of the pie remaining that the other party could possibly receive. This is referred to as distributive negotiation (Beersma & De Dreu, 2002; Thompson et al., 2010).

The way the Lannisters negotiate in the show largely demonstrates this type of negotiation. At least, the way they negotiate demonstrates that they have a mindset that negotiations can only be distributive. For instance, whenever Tyrion

Bend the Knee or Seize the Throne: Leadership Lessons from the Seven Kingdoms, 67–74
Copyright © 2023 by Nathan Tong and Michael J. Urick
Published under exclusive licence by Emerald Publishing Limited
doi:10.1108/978-1-80262-647-620231010

Lannister encounters a situation in which he needs to get his ideal outcome, his favorite tactic is simply to throw money at it. When he tries to get out of his prison in the Sky Cells in the Eyrie, he offers gold to Mord, the dim-witted guard. When he needs a swordsman to protect him, he offers Bronn a sum of money. When Cersei Lannister wants something, she tries her best to conserve as much of her resources (e.g., money, energy, efforts) as possible while attempting to get the biggest piece of "pie" possible for herself. For instance, when her father Tywin threatens to marry her off to Loras Tyrell, she threatens to ruin him (and the entire Lannister dynasty) by revealing her true relationship with her brother Jamie rather than trying to collaborate with Tywin to find a better, more optimal solution to keep their family in power. Jamie behaves the same way as his siblings when he tries to negotiate. Any time he is captured (e.g., by Catelyn Stark, by Locke under Roose Bolton's orders), he tries to talk his way out of imprisonment by offering his captors something of value in exchange for his freedom, resulting in what he believes is a 50/50 split of a whole "pie." What the Lannisters have in common is that they see negotiation opportunities as being purely distributive. They see resources as being fixed such that what one person gains, the other person loses.

However, in contrast to the way the Lannisters approach their negotiations, negotiations can also be over resources that can expand in value for each party. In these types of negotiations, called integrative negotiation (Beersma & De Dreu, 2002; Thompson et al., 2010), the negotiating parties get creative by optimizing every possible resource at each party's disposal, leaving no resource unexplored. Resources are used, combined, and recombined in an effort to make 1+1=3 rather than 2.

Jon Snow is an example of a character who approaches his negotiations with the belief that they can always be integrative rather than distributive. One of the missions of the men of the Night's Watch is to defend Castle Black against the Wildlings, because they are thought of as an enemy. However, when both the Night's Watch and the Wildlings need to survive against impending attack from the White Walkers, Jon negotiates with leaders from both the Night's Watch and the Wildlings for the Wildlings to be allowed to enter Castle Black. He has to work with Tormund Giantsbane to convince him and the rest of the Wildlings (the Free Folk) that having them enter Castle Black is not a trap, because they do not trust Jon after he kills Mance Rayder (although Jon did it out of mercy). On the other side, Jon points out to men of the Night's Watch that if the Wildlings remain in the North, they would be killed and then resurrected as White Walkers, which would add countless more soldiers to the Army of the Dead, which would make things exponentially more difficult for the men of the Night's Watch. Normally, the Wildlings passing through the gates of Castle Black would be a win–lose situation because, as enemies, one side would come out victorious while the other side would lose. But with Jon's negotiation, this becomes a win–win situation because the Wildlings are able to survive, Castle Black is better defended, and (as a third win) the Army of the Dead does not continue to grow.

The Stages of Negotiation

Processes usually have stages, and the negotiation process is no exception. Researchers have proposed that the negotiation process has four distinct stages:

relational positioning, identifying the problem, generating solutions, and reaching agreement (Adair & Brett, 2005). In this section, we will explore each of the four stages of negotiation, using the negotiation between Daenerys Targaryen and Kraznys mo Nakloz as she attempts to buy the Army of the Unsullied to illustrate each of the four stages of negotiation.

In the first stage, relational positioning, each party works to establish an understanding of where they stand with the other party (or parties) in terms of power and status. Do they have more power than the other party? Does the other party see them as a competitor or a collaborator? How much information can or should be revealed to the other party? As this stage progresses, each party gains a better understanding of their position in the negotiation process, as well as that of the other party(ies) involved. This understanding is important because it provides information about how much (or how little) influence and power one's party can exert over the negotiation, as well as how much (or how little) reciprocation can be expected between parties.

After arriving in Astapor, Daenerys wants to buy the entire Unsullied army, which consists of 8,000 fully trained soldiers. Kraznys mo Nakloz, the leader (or, more precisely, master) of the Unsullied, knows the value of his Unsullied soldiers, and he is not about to give them up without receiving something he believes is of similar (or greater) value in return. It is important to note here that Missandei assists in this process as a translator; her translation plays a key role in this first stage of the negotiation. As research suggests, the first stage of the negotiation between Daenerys and Kraznys is relational positioning. We see this play out as both parties assess one another through their dialogue. At this point, Daenerys needs as many soldiers as she can get as she continues to build her army to take the Iron Throne. She begins the negotiation by saying she wants to buy all 8,000 men. In doing so, she is testing Kraznys. How would he respond to this request? Would he entertain the idea? Would he sell every Unsullied solider he has? His initial response is to ensure that he heard her correctly, that she wants to buy all 8,000 men, which she confirms.

In his mind, Kraznys does not believe that Daenerys can afford to buy the entire Unsullied army. He proceeds to insult her by calling her a derogatory term and saying she does not have the means to pay for all 8,000 soldiers. Being diplomatic, Missandei translates most of what Kraznys says from Valyrian to the Common Tongue in the politest manner possible. Unfortunately for Kraznys, what he does not realize is that Daenerys fully understands what he's saying. Her native language is Valyrian, but as part of her strategy in the relational positioning stage of this negotiation, she keeps this information from Kraznys, not revealing that she can fully understand every word he says. As the dialogue continues, Daenerys confirms for herself that Kraznys does not think much of her, that he sees himself as being superior to her. He insults her by undervaluing everything she has to offer to pay for the 8,000 Unsullied soldiers. Daenerys plays along with Kraznys, pretending to use Missandei's translations to negotiate a deal when, in fact, she knows that Kraznys looks down at her and believes that he has more power, and thus more control, than she does over the negotiation.

However, while the dialogue is happening, Daenerys begins to form a strategy. Because she has dragons, she knows she actually has more negotiating power than

Kraznys. In other words, during this stage of relational positioning, Daenerys has figured out her position in the negotiation relative to the standing Kraznys has, based on what he is saying and how he is saying it, along with her knowledge of her full set of resources. However, Daenerys waits until what she believes is the right time during the negotiation process to reveal her information about her additional resources: her dragons.

The second stage of the negotiation process is identifying the problem. This stage involves detailed discussions and information exchanges between the parties. Depending on the amount of mutual trust built in the first stage, this second stage should, ideally, contain a reciprocal exchange of information between the parties that highlights each party's priorities and interests. In doing this, the parties will ideally reinforce, and continue to build, their mutual trust so that the parties can collaborate to achieve the most optimal outcome for all parties.

Kraznys, through his words, demonstrates that he thinks very little of Daenerys, and Daenerys learns that she cannot trust him. In this negotiation between Daenerys and Kraznys, there is little trust built in the first stage. Thus, in the second stage of this negotiation, the problem is further identified while information is exchanged in good faith. At the most basic level, the problem in this negotiation is that Daenerys wants to buy all 8,000 Unsullied soldiers, but she (initially) has nothing to offer that Kraznys believes to be at least equal in value to his men. Some of the information that is exchanged during this dialogue includes: Daenerys wants all 8,000 fully trained Unsullied soldiers, along with all the boys in training; Daenerys will only take all of them or there is no deal; Kraznys will give her only 100 Unsullied soldiers in exchange for her ship; and the remaining gold Daenerys has will normally buy her only 10 Unsullied soldiers, but Kraznys generously offers to give her 20 Unsullied soldiers. Kraznys offers additional information that the boys in training cannot be purchased because if they fail in battle, they will bring shame to Astapor. After Daenerys understands that Kraznys thinks very little of her by insulting her with his exchange offers, she decides that it is a good idea to share with him her additional piece of information: she has dragons. This piques his interest because dragons have not been seen for thousands of years and, for Kraznys, dragons are more valuable than his Unsullied men. Daenerys' presentation of this information to Kraznys opens the door for the third stage of this negotiation.

Stage three of the negotiation process is characterized by the generation of solutions. This stage can be energizing and passionate (Adair & Brett, 2005) because during this stage, the parties are working together to find the most optimal solution for everyone involved while incorporating all the "must-haves" for each party, and simultaneously trying to make an impact on the outcome. During this stage, each party considers any offers that are presented, trying to figure out whether the offers meet their needs, how much it aligns with and optimizes their goals, and how to possibly get the other party to sweeten the deal even more.

After learning that Daenerys has dragons, Kraznys offers a solution for Daenerys to solve her "problem" of not having enough money or goods to pay for the 8,000 Unsullied soldiers and the boys in training. In a very rapid back and forth exchange, Kraznys requests three dragons in exchange for the Army of the

Unsullied along with the boys in training, to which Daenerys responds, "One." Kraznys quickly reduces his offer to two, but Daenerys holds firm to her offer of just one dragon. Kraznys reluctantly agrees to the offer of one dragon, but he requests that he receives the biggest dragon. Daenerys swiftly replies, "Done." And with this, the negotiation moves into its last stage.

The fourth and final stage in the negotiation process is reaching an agreement. In this stage, the details of the negotiation are finalized, and the parties make an agreement about what each party will give and receive. Certainly, this stage can also be reached if the parties discover in the previous stage that reaching an agreement is just not possible, resulting in an impasse. However, because of all the time and effort invested in the three previous stages, the parties can be confident that any agreement they reach in the fourth stage is not only acceptable, but also the most optimal.

The final agreement between Daenerys and Kraznys is that he will receive Daenerys' largest dragon in exchange for his 8,000 Unsullied soldiers plus all the boys in training. However, Daenerys adds an additional condition to their agreement. Because she knows (from the first stage) that she is in a position of power in this negotiation, she requests for one more thing from Kraznys: ownership of Missandei, as a token of a well-struck bargain. Although his agreement to this request is not shown, the scene cuts to Daenerys walking and talking with Missandei, indicating that Kraznys agreed to this final request in the negotiation.

While there are distinguishable stages during a negotiation, they do not always occur so neatly and discretely. In other words, the stages can and often do blend into one another. For instance, during the negotiation between Daenerys and Kraznys, there is relational positioning (the first stage) occurring while the two parties are generating solutions (the third stage). While discussing possible solutions to the problem of Daenerys not having anything that Kraznys values (except for the dragons), Daenerys continually processes the unspoken information Kraznys conveys (via his words, his tone of voice, his facial expressions, for instance). Through the subtext from the words he speaks and how he expresses himself, Daenerys can tell what he thinks about his perception of each of their positions, in terms of their power in this negotiation (he thinks he has all the power and she has none).

Although Daenerys undermines the negotiation (because she knows her dragon cannot be enslaved), this scenario is an example of integrative negotiation. Instead of limiting the resources used to reach an agreement, Daenerys expands the "pie" that is under negotiation. The two parties could have talked in circles for days or weeks (if not longer) trying to come to an agreement about how many ships and how much gold it would take to buy as many Unsullied men as possible and what that final number would be. However, Daenerys incorporates other resources available to both parties into the negotiation, including the boys in training and her dragons. Instead of bargaining with just the obvious resources at each party's disposal, which would limit the scope of the negotiation (i.e., it would limit the size of the "pie"), Daenerys successfully attempts to expand the negotiation so that each party walks away with more than they originally thought they could.

Potential Biases in Negotiation

One notable aspect of this particular negotiation is that there is likely an underlying diversity issue that influences behaviors, especially those of Kraznys. Generally, during negotiations, personal biases can be activated that then often lead to discriminatory behaviors being enacted (Ayres, 1991; Hoffman & Triantafillou, 2014). These biases can lead to one party treating another party (or other parties) as though they are less than equals during the negotiation process, which is exactly what Kraznys does as he negotiates with Daenerys. These biases can stem from a variety of factors such as age, gender, language or accent, race or ethnicity, cultural background, sexual orientation, disability, religion, or numerous other factors. In this case, Kraznys perceives Daenerys as simple and ignorant, likely because she is a woman, she is small in stature, and she does not speak Valyrian (or so he thinks). Biased attitudes and their resulting behaviors can harm negotiations because one party might take advantage of the other (or others), just as we witness Kraznys try to do with Daenerys their negotiation over the Army of the Unsullied. Unfortunately, these behaviors can and do happen in real-world negotiations, and they can negatively impact the outcomes of negotiations, regardless of whether they are done unconsciously or intentionally. Thus, when business leaders enter into a negotiation, they must be aware of their personal biases so that they do not allow them to manifest as discriminatory behaviors that can ultimately negatively impact the outcomes of negotiations.

Negotiation Tactics

There are several tactics that research has shown to be important in impacting the outcomes of negotiations. Among these are negotiating multiple issues at the same time, concessions and reciprocation, and issue-based tactics (Geiger, 2017; Hüffmeier et al., 2014).

One tactic that has been shown to improve outcomes for all parties during negotiation is negotiating multiple issues simultaneously instead of discussing them one at a time individually (Froman & Cohen, 1970; Thompson et al., 1988). Doing this allows the parties of the negotiation to simultaneously work competitively and collaboratively (Mannix et al., 1989). When the parties in a negotiation discuss and consider one issue at a time, the focus of the bargaining and discussion unfortunately becomes that specific issue rather than the overall goal of the negotiation (Mannix et al., 1989). In turn, focusing on individual issues tends to result in suboptimal outcomes for everyone involved in the negotiation (Mannix et al., 1989). However, many studies on negotiation have presented participants only a few issues at a time for the parties to negotiate (e.g., three issues; Patton & Balakrishnan, 2010) whereas in real negotiations, the number of issues under consideration can be significantly greater. Thus, the effect of negotiating numerous issues simultaneously remains unclear.

Petyr Baelish, also called Littlefinger, is masterful in his use of this tactic. Some examples of when we see this includes when he is negotiating with the Tyrells and the Lannisters to unite the houses, with the Lords of the Vale about Lysa Arryn's death and what is to become of her son Robin, and with Roose Bolton about Sansa Stark's fate after their plans to wed her to Ramsay Bolton. Littlefinger is smart and careful to not focus his negotiations on any one topic at one time. Instead, in order to get the outcomes he wants, he makes his arguments using several different but related issues simultaneously, which makes his negotiation partners view the bigger picture and, thus, focus the end result, rather than on individual discussion points.

Making concessions and showing reciprocal behaviors have also proven to affect negotiations (Hüffmeier et al., 2014). Behaviors such as ambitious first offers can benefit the party that makes that initial offer (Galinsky & Mussweiler, 2001), but doing so in repeated negotiations can have the reverse effect (Cotter & Henley, 2008). Researchers have found that when there is a sense of give-and-take between the parties, it makes the negotiation a more transparent interaction, resulting in a heightened awareness for each party of how much (or how little) they are reciprocating the concessionary behavior (Hüffmeier et al., 2014). If one party perceives that another party is not mirroring their concessionary behavior, they tend to see this behavior as unfair. If they decide to then take a firm stance in the negotiation (in response to the perceived unfair behavior), it can result in a downward spiral which then leads to suboptimal outcomes for all parties (Hüffmeier et al., 2014). (See Chapter 9 for a more in-depth exploration of fairness.)

In *Game of Thrones*, we see Jon Snow make a concession by bending the knee to Daenerys. He and Daenerys had been in negotiations for some time because he is trying to guarantee her help in fighting the Army of the Dead. Their negotiation had been going on for a while, and Jon realizes he cannot defeat the Army of the Dead without her help. Thus, he bends the knee as a concession in order to get Daenerys to help him defend the North.

There are also tactics that involve focusing on one specific issue in the negotiation in order to gain a benefit. Two examples of these tactics are phony issues and nibble tactics (Shell, 2006). With a phony issue, a party will bring up an issue that is of little significance to them but exaggerate its importance. Then, by making a concession on this exaggerated issue, they can gain concessions from the other party (because of an expectation of reciprocal behaviors) on issues that are actually important to them. Nibble tactics are used after an agreement has been settled by the parties. They involve requesting one last small concession at or just before closing the agreement. Because of their small size, they typically do not jeopardize the negotiation, but they can upset the opposing party (Lewicki et al., 2010).

Examples of both phony issues and a nibble tactic can be found in the negotiation between Daenerys and Kraznys. The phony issue is the dragon that Daenerys agrees to exchange for the Unsullied army. She knows that her biggest dragon, named Drogon, cannot be enslaved and that he will only listen to her. When Daenerys hands Drogon over to Kraznys in exchange for the whip that controls the Unsullied soldiers, both parties have technically fulfilled their respective agreements in the negotiation. However, Daenerys knows Kraznys will not be able to control Drogon, and she instructs Drogon to set Kraznys ablaze, killing him and leaving her as master of the Army of the Unsullied. The nibble tactic in this negotiation is ownership of Missandei. What's under negotiation are the 8,000 Unsullied men and the boys in training. After the agreement is made to exchange the Unsullied and the boys for one dragon, Daenerys requests ownership of Missandei. As one single slave, Missandei does not endanger the agreement because, in terms of her relative value compared to what is under negotiation, she is insignificant.

Summary

Negotiations are necessary for leaders and managers to get others to work toward organizational goals. And for better or for worse, negotiations are unavoidable for leaders and managers. Thus, when approaching negotiations, leaders should keep in mind that:

- Negotiations are not "fights," but instead are opportunities for parties to work together to achieve and attain more together through an agreement than they would without the agreement.
- Negotiations have four distinct stages: relational positioning, problem identification, generating solutions, and reaching agreement. The first three stages often, but do not always, occur in this order.
- There are tactics that have been shown to improve outcomes in negotiation including discussing multiple issues simultaneously, making concessions and showing reciprocal behavior, emphasizing phony issues, and engaging in nibble tactics.

Negotiations can only occur when there are two or more parties involved. Increasingly, those parties can come from different parts of the world, trying to negotiate for resources they cannot obtain in their own country. As organizational managers and leaders, it is important to understand the perspectives of one's negotiation partners, especially when they come from a culture different than one's own. Thus, in the next chapter, we explore cultural awareness and sensitivity.

Chapter 11

Cultural Awareness and Sensitivity

As businesses become increasingly integrated around the world, managers and organizations would do well to be culturally aware if they want to be or remain successful. Organizations that want to source the most cost-effective materials, recruit and maintain the most qualified and talented employees, and/or operate their business internationally should do their best to ensure that their managers and leaders are culturally aware and culturally sensitive. Being sensitive to differences in cultures from around the world, or even to the smaller cultural differences within larger cultures (e.g., local or regional cultures within a national culture), helps managers to avoid missteps with words and/or actions that can come across as ignorant, inconsiderate, rude, or even offensive when working with others. This is particularly important when working for the first time with those who come from a different culture.

In addition to avoiding embarrassing or disrespectful comments or behaviors, being culturally aware and culturally sensitive can provide a host of benefits, such as learning to value others and their perspectives, reducing stereotypes that can be limiting, expanding understanding of oneself and others, and appreciating the non-verbal communication that teaches us what it means to be human beings (Congdon, 1984). In this chapter, we will discuss what culture is and examine how some of the characters in *Game of Thrones* benefited from being culturally aware and culturally sensitive, and how other characters in the show faced the consequences of their lack of cultural awareness and sensitivity.

What is Culture?

Before diving into the importance of cultural awareness and sensitivity, we need to briefly examine what culture is. According to Geert Hofstede, one of the foremost culture researchers, culture is "the collective programming of the mind that distinguishes the members of one group or category of people from others" (Hofstede, 2011, p. 3). In other words, culture is how people perceive and make sense of the world, and that perspective distinguishes them as part of, and apart from, a certain group. These groups are often referred to as tribes, nations, or organizations, and culture can be applied to any group, for instance, groups based on gender, sexual orientation, age or generation, race or ethnicity, and societal

Bend the Knee or Seize the Throne: Leadership Lessons from the Seven Kingdoms, 75–82
Copyright © 2023 by Nathan Tong and Michael J. Urick
Published under exclusive licence by Emerald Publishing Limited
doi:10.1108/978-1-80262-647-620231011

class, just to name a few (Hofstede, 2011). In short, culture can refer to any collection of individuals who have a shared mindset. This mindset creates a set of shared values, norms, assumptions, and general patterns of behavior among the members of that culture (Govindarajan & Gupta, 2001).

Because culture is a "programming of the mind," or, in other words, a mindset, it influences the way individuals within a culture think about and perceive the world, such as their behaviors, perceptions, and expectations. Thus, it can be difficult to explain one's culture to someone from outside that culture. Take your own culture as an example. Why are certain things the way they are? In your culture, why is it necessary (or unnecessary) to greet the salesperson at a store? Why do you eat with utensils rather than with your hands (or vice versa)? Why do you leave a tip (or not) for your server at a restaurant? The answer to these questions might seem obvious to you because you are a member of your culture, but how would you explain the norms, values, and perceptions in your answers to these questions to someone from a different culture, especially if that person comes from a culture where the norms and values are completely the opposite of those in your culture? As you can probably see, culture is very powerful because it impacts how people think and behave.

In *Game of Thrones*, the Lannisters have a strong culture of making sure that they get their way during their interactions with others at almost any cost, as well as a strong culture of valuing wealth, power, and family above all else. It would likely be extremely difficult for them to explain their culture to others. It is how their minds are programmed; it's how they think. They don't put any conscious effort into maintaining or reinforcing their perspective; it's just how their brains are wired to work to think about and view the world. As Tyrion Lannister conveys in the first season, nobody turns away a Lannister. The way the Lannisters (i.e., Tywin, Jamie, Cersei, and Tyrion) behave among themselves and while interacting with others provides those outside the Lannister clan, including us as viewers, a glimpse into their culture. But is behavior the only way to discern what a culture entails? Luckily, the answer is "no." There are other cultural elements that can be used.

Cultural Elements

Fortunately for those who want to learn about cultures other than their own, cultures manifest themselves in the form of cultural elements (Harton & Bourgeois, 2003). Some examples of cultural elements include a population's attitudes, beliefs, language, and physical artifacts. Language as a cultural element is manifested in how thoughts are expressed and how words are used in a culture. As a real-world example of language as a cultural element, we can take a look at the English word "hello" and its translations in other languages. These translations might include *hola* in Spanish, *bonjour* in French, *buongiorno* in Italian, and *hallo* in Norwegian. We might even translate it to *ni hao* in Chinese or *kon'nichiwa* in Japanese. However, these last two are not entirely accurate and do not necessarily reflect how the people in those cultures write or pronounce these words. In terms of writing, these cultures use different characters that are not based on the

Latin alphabet to write these words in their language, as we have done here. And in terms of pronunciation, the equivalent translations here are merely phonetic imitations that do not capture the cultural nuances behind these words (e.g., how, when, why, and with whom they are used).

In *Game of Thrones*, a striking example of language as a cultural element is the Dothraki language. The way the Dothraki people express themselves and communicate with each other in their language with their words is an element of their culture. One cultural element in particular is very telling about the way the Dothraki people view the world: they do not have a way to say "thank you." Ser Jorah Mormont explains this to Daenerys Targaryen as she learns Dothraki language and culture after being married to Khal Drogo. As this cultural element suggests, the Dothraki people most likely do not feel gratitude toward others in their culture, as indicated by the fact that they do not have a way to convey this sentiment, at least not verbally. If gratitude were an emotion they experienced regularly (or at all), or at least something they felt the need to express to others, then they would have come up with a word, a phrase, or some sort of physical gesture or action to be able to convey this sentiment among themselves. But because no method exists for the Dothraki to say thank you or otherwise express gratitude, we can surmise from this cultural element that gratitude is not something the people from the Dothraki culture feel, perceive, or experience.

Certainly, the Dothraki people, their culture, and their language are fictional, but in the real world, there are many examples of language serving as an element of culture. For example, many Asian (national) cultures, such as those of Japan and China, use language that is infused with meaning and subtext (Broeder, 2021). In these cultures, the speaker and the context tend to convey far more to the audience than content of the message itself (Broeder, 2021). In contrast, the language of many Western (national) cultures, such as those of the USA and Germany, are much more straightforward. The content of communication in these cultures tends to be more important than who is conveying the message. (See Chapter 5 for a more detailed discussion about communication.)

Another example of cultural elements are physical artifacts. Physical artifacts are material manifestations of the way the people in a culture think and behave. They can include items such as designs and tools that convey what the people of a culture value, how their world functions, and how they live their daily lives. In *Game of Thrones*, the house banners and the sigils on them are examples of physical artifacts that not only demonstrate the culture of each house, but also the culture of the people of Westeros. For instance, the sigil of House Bolton is a white X against a black background, with an upside-down man with his flesh exposed. As a cultural element, this sigil conveys to others that a large part of the culture of the Boltons is being unafraid to face their enemies and they will kill their enemies by flaying them. The sigil of House Greyjoy shows a golden kraken on a black background. The members of House Greyjoy come from the Iron Islands and, thus, much of their culture has to do with the seas. For instance, they are particularly skilled with their ships. It makes sense, then, that one of their most important cultural elements, their house sigil, contains an image related to the seas.

The banners themselves also convey the culture of the people of the Seven Kingdoms of Westeros. Even young children in Westeros are taught to memorize and recognize the house banners and sigils, as we saw Arya Stark doing in the first season of the show. This is an important part of the culture in Westeros because recognizing house banners could mean the difference between living and dying. Zooming out a bit more, the fact that these banners are even necessary in this culture tells us something about the culture of Westeros, such as that their identification with their house is important to them as a people and they need to be able to quickly recognize friend from foe.

As one last example of a physical artifact from *Game of Thrones*, consider the pin that signifies the wearer as the Hand of the King, the second most important position in Westeros after the monarch. This pin entitles its bearer to many privileges and responsibilities as Hand of the King. We see this pin on Ned Stark, Jamie Lannister, Tywin Lannister, Tyrion Lannister, Kevan Lannister, and Qyburn, all of whom have served as Hand of the King (or Queen) at some point in the series. As a testament to how significant this pin is, in the final season of the show, we see Tyrion rip off the pin and throw it on the ground in protest of Daenerys burning down King's Landing. In doing this, he is signaling, as strongly as he can, his protest of Daenerys's actions and, consequently, his resignation as Hand of the Queen to Daenerys. He could have just walked away from her or verbally resigned from his position, but instead, he chooses to engage in this action of removing the pin and throwing it away. Certainly, this is done in part for dramatic effect for the show, but it also demonstrates the importance of cultural artifacts and the significance and meaning they can convey to the people of a culture.

In short, cultural elements are those pieces of a culture that can be qualified and/or quantified. That is, unlike culture itself, which is a mindset, cultural elements can be assigned some sort of definition and/or measurement. When an outsider encounters elements from an unfamiliar culture, these elements can provide them with bits of knowledge about that culture to gain a better understanding of it. In *Game of Thrones*, there are numerous cultural elements aside from language, sigils, banners, and pins; there are also clothing, hairstyles, titles, and weapons, just to name a few. Cultural elements can give us a glimpse into a culture, but unless someone is from that specific culture, they will almost never fully understand that foreign culture, no matter how many cultural elements they encounter or examine.

Why Cultural Awareness and Sensitivity Matter

Because people from outside a specific culture will almost never be able to fully understand it, it is important to, first, be aware that cultural differences exist and, second, be sensitive to the nuances of a culture in order to be able to most effectively interact with its people. Note that cultural awareness is only the first step. The next step that is crucial to take is having cultural sensitivity, which is defined as a willingness to accept that the differences between cultures all have equal merit (Hart et al., 2019). By being culturally sensitive when working in a group with people from another culture (or multiple other cultures), one can better cultivate trust, understanding, and cohesiveness among group members (Govindarajan & Gupta, 2001). Taking the time to understand and appreciate different cultures, which in part includes learning the significance behind a culture's elements, can provide people with insights into those unfamiliar cultures to better interpret and understand the values, norms, and behaviors of people from that culture. In the next sections, we will explore the advantages of being culturally aware and culturally sensitive, as well as the negative consequences of not doing so.

The Benefits of Cultural Awareness and Sensitivity

As we mentioned above, being culturally aware and practicing cultural sensitivity can help build trust, understanding, and cohesiveness in groups with people from different cultures (Govindarajan & Gupta, 2001). In doing so, one can learn to value others and their differing perspectives, increase one's understanding of the world, and garner benefits that may not otherwise have been available. When we look at the world only through our own cultural lens, the world tends to be black and white with limited shades of gray. Through cultural sensitivity, numerous new shades of gray, and potentially many new colors never seen before, become available to us. Perspectives become expanded and new thoughts, as well as new ways of thinking, are born when the shackles and limitations of one's cultural viewpoints are removed.

Another benefit of being culturally aware and keenly culturally sensitive is high cultural intelligence, or CQ, which scholars have defined as "a person's capability for successful adaptation to new cultural settings" (Earley & Ang, 2003, p. 59). Generally, CQ encompasses a person's knowledge of the cultural environment in which they find themself; their mental capacity to learn, understand, and use cultural knowledge; and the degree to which they can act appropriately, demonstrate flexibility, and adapt their behaviors to reflect their current cultural situation (Ang et al., 2007; Earley & Ang, 2003). This is especially important for businesses and organizations that want to trade or operate internationally. To successfully conduct business in countries where the culture is different, or with its citizens, adaptation and flexibility in terms of culture are paramount. To not be adaptable and flexible could lead to egregious errors that can insult or even offend the members of that foreign culture. For business managers who invest organizational resources in developing their employees' CQ, the investment has numerous advantages (Earley & Ang, 2003). Having employees with high CQ can offer organizations a chance to reap benefits such as expanded and enduring business partnerships, enlarged networks, and new opportunities that may have previously been unrecognized, among other benefits that can stem from trust that is built as a result of high CQ.

In *Game of Thrones*, Jon Snow is culturally aware and very culturally sensitive. Whether he is working with low-status people like the Free Folk (the Wildlings), high-status people like the Lannisters, or even his own men of the Night's Watch, he acknowledges that each group has its own culture, and he adapts his words and behaviors to align with the norms and rules of that culture. As an example, after some of the Free Folk are killed and captured by Stannis Baratheon's army, Jon visits Tormund Giantsbane, one of the Free Folk, to let him know that their bodies are going to be burned, and he asks whether Tormund would like him to say any words (to honor those who were killed). Tormund is confused and asks what words Jon means. Jon then tells him he means funeral words, and that he is asking because he doesn't know how the Free Folk say farewell to their dead. Tormund tells Jon that the dead cannot hear them, meaning there is nothing Jon needs to do for the Free Folk who were killed. (Notice that this is a cultural element of the Free Folk, manifested as a perspective about and an attitude toward the dead.) The fact that Jon takes the time to ask these questions shows that he is not only aware that the Free Folk have a distinct culture, but he also has cultural sensitivity. He wants to make sure he takes care of the bodies of the deceased Free Folk in the same way they would in their own culture. Tormund then tells Jon that Ygritte really did love him and insinuates that he can respect their culture while demonstrating his true feelings for Ygritte by returning her body north of the Wall. Jon does this and lays her to rest by burning her body in the forest north of the Wall.

Jon's actions in these scenes demonstrate that he acknowledges the culture of the Free Folk and that they may honor their dead by conducting their funerals differently than what he is accustomed to in his culture. In other words, he is culturally aware. He also exhibits cultural sensitivity by asking Tormund what he should say when they burn the bodies of the fall Free Folk, and by doing what the Free Folk would have done for Ygritte. In this case, Tormund tells Jon that Ygritte belongs in the North, and Jon practices cultural sensitivity by carrying her body north of the Wall and burning it there. It is, in part, actions and behaviors like Jon's in situations like this that make people see him as a leader. He wants to do right by whomever he is working with, and one way to do this is to not only be culturally aware, but also practice cultural sensitivity.

The Downside of Not Being Culturally Aware or Sensitive

Although there is a saying that ignorance is bliss, nothing could be further from the truth when it comes to cultural awareness and cultural sensitivity. Lacking cultural awareness and/or cultural sensitivity, regardless of whether it's intentional or accidental, can lead to a host of problems, especially in business (Govindarajan & Gupta, 2001). Negotiations can stall or be terminated, business deals can fall through, and even partnerships can turn sour if one party feels slighted by another because of perceived violations of culture based on people's words and/or actions, even if they are unintentional. At a very basic level, these perceived offenses can stem from miscommunication or misunderstandings, norm infringements, and values violations.

There is at least one character in *Game of Thrones* who, unfortunately, suffers the consequences of not being culturally aware or sensitive: Viserys Targaryen. In the first season of the show, Viserys brokers a deal to marry off his sister Daenerys to Khal Drogo, one of the leaders of the Dothraki. In exchange, he will receive an army of Dothraki soldiers to help him in his quest to reclaim the Iron Throne, which he claims to have lost after his father, Aerys II, the "Mad King," is murdered. After her marriage to Drogo, Daenerys is referred to as Khaleesi by the Dothraki, a title that roughly translates to *queen* and gives her power among the Dothraki people. (Notice that this title is a cultural element.)

During their travels, Daenerys, as a new khaleesi, orders the party to come to a halt. This command angers Viserys because he sees himself, and not his little sister (whom he uses simply as a bartering tool), as the person who gives orders. In his anger, he draws his sword at Daenerys. In response, Daenerys' newly appointed bodyguard (given to her because she is a khaleesi) disarms Viserys and offers to kill him for Daenerys, to which she says no. After this incident, the Dothraki take away the horse that Viserys was riding and force him to walk alongside the group, like their servants and slaves do.

Several aspects of the Dothraki culture are on display in this incident, and Viserys violates many norms of their culture, to his detriment. We can see through this incident that the Dothraki people value hierarchy. According to Dothraki culture, each person's title and position in their society dictates their lot in life, such as what rights and privileges they are entitled to, whether they have servants, and even whether they can ride a horse. When Viserys draws his sword and threatens Daenerys, he directly violates Dothraki culture, specifically the importance of recognizing and respecting hierarchy. As a result of his actions, Viserys has his horse taken away from him and he is forced to walk alongside the group like one the servants.

Throughout the first season of the show, Viserys sees the Dothraki people as just a tool for him to use to reclaim the Iron Throne. Unlike Daenerys, he does not take the time or make the effort to try to learn Dothraki culture. He does not acknowledge that they have a culture different from his own as a Targaryen. In other words, he does not seem to be culturally aware and, if he is, he does not practice cultural sensitivity. We can tell from his words, behaviors, and attitude that he essentially does not see the Dothraki as people nor does he value their worth. He feels he is superior to them, often referring to himself as "The Dragon," which, in his culture, represents him being superior to everyone else, including his sister Daenerys.

In his final scene in the show, Viserys bursts into a tent where the Dothraki are having a feast, draws his sword again on Daenerys (again, whom he sees as just little sister, but whom the Dothraki view as a khaleesi), and demands from Drogo that he gets the crown he was promised from their bargain. His behavior in this scene violates many aspects of Dothraki culture and is seen by the Dothraki as rude, disrespectful, and offensive. (Likely, Viserys' behavior in this scene is considered rude, disrespectful, and offensive in many different real-world cultures.) Because of Viserys's behavior, Khal Drogo melts down his belt made of gold and pours it on Viserys's head as his crown, killing him.

In real-world negotiations and business partnerships, nobody dies like Viserys did when cultural norms are violated. However, deals and negotiations can take a turn for the worse and actual and potential partnerships can meet their demise if cultural awareness and cultural sensitivity are not considered and practiced when working with people from different cultures.

One additional aspect about culture that culturally aware and culturally sensitive business managers and leaders should keep in mind is that cultures can and do change over time due to issues like population fluctuations (Shennen, 2000), environmental factors (e.g., agricultural; Dean et al., 2000), and technological advances (Fox, 2018). Because the world is constantly changing and evolving, cultural norms, preferences, and tastes can shift. What was once acceptable in a culture may now have fallen out of fashion or favor among members of a culture. Thus, part of being culturally sensitive and having high CQ includes maintaining awareness of any shifts or changes in a culture.

Summary

As we have seen in this chapter, it is important for organizations and their members to not only be culturally aware, but they must also be culturally sensitive if they hope to successfully operate their business internationally or with international partners and stakeholders. Business managers and leaders must keep the following in mind:

- Clues about a culture can be gleaned from cultural elements, but cultural elements cannot convey all the nuances of a culture.
- Cultural awareness and cultural sensitivity can foster a host of benefits including building mutual trust, appreciation, and respect among people from different cultural backgrounds.
- Not recognizing or appreciating cultural differences can be detrimental to organizations; they can impede or even harm business deals, negotiations, and partnerships.
- Cultures can change over time, so practicing cultural sensitivity and having high CQ includes keeping up with any cultural changes that might occur.

We have covered a lot of ground about culture in this chapter, and a lot of different management and leadership topics in this book. In the next and final chapter, we revisit these topics to reinforce the importance of each and every aspect we have discussed.

Chapter 12

Conclusion

Throughout the Seven Kingdoms, kings, queens, knights, bastards, and common-ers all must choose whether to bend the knee and defer to another leader's rule or to attempt to seize the throne to rule Westeros. While many may be interested in the latter, only one person may sit on the Iron Throne at a time, just as normally only one person may be the CEO of an organization.

Yet, even without the title of King or Queen, many characters in *Game of Thrones* exert influence and make decisions, just like their monarch does. There-fore, there are leaders throughout the Seven Kingdoms in addition to the one person who sits on the Iron Throne. Throughout this book, we have examined many of these leaders in Westeros. In this final concluding chapter, we offer some of our perspectives and trends we noted through our exploration of some of the many leaders in the Seven Kingdoms.

Effective Queens and Kings Understand Their Context to Inform Their Leadership Styles and Activities of Making Decisions, Communicating, and Motivating in Order to Achieve Common Goals

Leaders engage in a variety of different activities. These, of course, include mak-ing decisions, interacting with other organizational stakeholders, and motivating followers. While some overconfident rulers of Westeros might be convinced that their way of engaging in each of these activities is the best way, they may be incor-rect. Through examining various types of leaderships, it is clear that there is not one "best" way of being a leader.

Instead, a leader must remain flexible. They must know (or learn) when to seek the input of followers before making decisions, but they must also know when they need to make an executive decision, potentially without as much input from followers, in order to move forward quickly through crisis situations.

Of course, followers' ability and willingness to engage in particular tasks, as well as a leader's relationship to each follower individually and the followers col-lectively, are part of the context. However, leaders must consider other aspects of their context including culture, workplace trends, their own knowledge and skills,

Bend the Knee or Seize the Throne: Leadership Lessons from the Seven Kingdoms, 83–89
Copyright © 2023 by Nathan Tong and Michael J. Urick
Published under exclusive licence by Emerald Publishing Limited
doi:10.1108/978-1-80262-647-620231012

and much more. A holistic understanding of their context will better inform a leader's approach to decision-making, communicating, and motivating.

The purpose, of course, of understanding context in order to adjust one's leadership style is to work toward achieving and accomplishing common goals shared by those in an organization. Without common goals to work toward, it will be difficult for leaders to motivate others and exert influence. Just think of the organization as a raft and every employee has a paddle. We might all be paddling, but we might not all be paddling in the same direction to get us to our collective desired destination. And while managers can get everyone paddling in the same direction, leaders get everyone to paddle in the same direction while simultaneously motivating everyone to paddle their best.

Effective Queens and Kings Know That the Traits and Behaviors that Helped Them Emerge as Leaders Will Not Necessarily Make Them Effective in Their Roles; Instead, They Learn from Challenges, Find Ways to Influence Others That Fit Their Context, and Continuously Adapt

Game of Thrones provides many different examples of how leaders emerge. Interestingly, through characters like Cersei Lannister, it is evident that those traits or characteristics that allow for a leader to emerge do not always lead to leadership success. In fact, these very things that contribute to leader emergence can cause that leader's downfall. Certainly, in *Game of Thrones*, some of the best leaders are those who have overcome challenges and tragedies. Through these experiences, they've developed the insight, understanding, and, at times, skills they need to be an effective leader.

Of course, successful leaders need to possess some traits that fit their role. However, they also have to have some base of power that allows them to be influential. These bases could be from their title, ability to reward or punish, expertise, or likeability. But regardless of which base(s) they possess, in order to be successful, their traits, behaviors, and modes of influence need to relate to their environment if they are to be effective.

But, it is also important to note that it is not enough for a leader to rest on their laurels once they've been (or become) successful. Their context is always changing; new challenges, pressures, technology, preferences, and the like can emerge that disrupt or completely change the current familiar environment. Therefore, those leaders who are able to effectively adapt to these changes are the ones who will best survive and thrive. And, in order to adapt, they must be open to learning throughout their careers.

Effective Queens and Kings Leverage Multiple Bases of Power, Often Alongside Servant or Transformational Leadership Approaches, in an Ethical Manner That is Focused on the Common Good

Speaking of ways in which leaders can build influence, there are at least five approaches as noted above. In Westeros, many of the would-be queens and kings rely on one or more of these approaches as they try to sway and influence their followers.

Those leaders who draw from multiple bases of power tend to be more successful than leaders who draw upon only one base of power. If these bases are used in conjunction with servant or transformational leadership styles of leadership, then those leaders who leverage these approaches are likely to be even more successful.

Yet, there is an ethical side to wielding power. Each of the bases of power could be used for a leader's own personal gain or to promote the common good. Those leaders who tend to focus on using their power for the betterment of others (such as Bran Stark and, after the beginning of the series, Tyrion Lannister), tend to fare better.

Effective Queens and Kings Communicate in a Manner That Accurately and Truthfully Conveys Meaning to Multiple Audiences

Kings and queens must also focus on how they communicate. Of course, all communicators engage in the process of intent, encoding, transmitting, receipt/decoding, and feedback. Likewise, all communicators, whether in modern organizations or in Westeros, can experience hindrances in conveying their meaning to others.

Just like in the Seven Kingdoms, modern organizations can see their leaders communicating with a variety of different styles. In order to be as effective as possible in communicating, leaders need to determine what communication style fits best with their context. Part of being an effective leader is to have an ability to speak and/or write in order to communicate a clear, consistent message to multiple audiences (all of whom may have differing perceptions and, therefore, differing reactions to a message) in a manner that allows for thorough understanding and, ultimately, complete comprehension.

In attempting to reach multiple audiences and adjusting their communication style, leaders should remain open and honest in their communication. Certainly, many leaders in Westeros are not open and/or honest, just as some leaders in our organizations are not, unfortunately. Yet, in *Game of Thrones*, it is often those leaders who distort a message's meaning or use communication purely for personal gain who end up not sitting on the Iron Throne for very long.

Effective Queens and Kings Thoroughly Understand the Values They Care About Most and Deliberately Use Them to Guide Their Decisions

Certainly, along with leveraging power and communicating, the leaders who seem to be more effective are those whose actions, decisions, and behaviors are driven by some sense of values and morals that are accepted by a broader group. Because leaders make many decisions, it is important that they have a clear understanding of the values that guide those decisions.

There are many different ethical frameworks that leaders might use to guide their decision-making. Some of these might include a desire to minimize pain, conform to a social group's standards, emphasize the importance of universal rights or duties, focus on the outcomes of a decision, understand the context, or draw upon one's faith-based values.

You probably recognize some leaders in your own organization who utilize one or more of these values-approaches in their decision-making, just as you likely now see these approaches in many of the characters in *Game of Thrones*. As you consider your own ethics and leadership style, you will likely want to reflect on what your values are so that you can make decisions deliberately with a concern for what you most care about. As leaders, we must also consider what we would do (or what we actually do) if and when our values conflict with the values of our followers.

Effective Queens and Kings Understand How to Motivate Followers

Leadership requires influencing followers to engage in desired behaviors which, in addition to possessing and using bases of influence, can be done through motivating followers. There are several approaches to motivating others that the characters in *Game of Thrones*, as well as our real-world leaders, have used or currently use.

One way of understanding motivation is that an individual will engage in a behavior if they believe the following two principles. First, trying (i.e., putting in effort) leads to engagement in some desired behavior. Second, performance of the desired behavior will lead to a positive consequence that holds some sort of value.

Likewise, individuals are motivated when they have goals to guide them. Motivation will be highest when the goals are clear and clearly articulated, when they are difficult (but not impossible) to obtain, when they are made public, and when feedback is provided along the way.

Effective Queens and Kings Know They Will Not Sit on the Throne for Long if Their Followers Do Not Trust Them, So They Actively Seek to Build and Maintain Trust

Trust is of the utmost importance when considering leadership. Regardless of one's formal title, leaders and followers inevitably become vulnerable to each other at some point in their relationship. Leaders need to believe that followers will do their jobs to the best of their ability. And followers need to believe that leaders are looking out for their best interests.

Leaders who do not convey, build, and maintain trust between and among followers will likely not sit on the Iron Throne, or in the corner office, for very long. Followers need to believe in their leaders in order to support them.

Though followers may show varying amounts of willingness to trust their leaders, leaders should still strive to build and maintain as much trust as possible.

Some ways they can do this involve demonstrating their ability, acting out of benevolence, and highlighting their integrity.

Effective Queens and Kings Understand That Perceptions of Fairness are Ultimately Linked to Their Ability to Influence

To be just means to give the appearance of being fair. Leaders who treat their followers fairly make them feel like they are a valued member of the group and belong within that group. This feeling of being valued and belonging leads to increased motivation and demonstration of beneficial prosocial behaviors. If a leader is perceived to be just, then they also may be more likely to exert a stronger level of influence on followers.

On the other hand, those leaders who are perceived to act unjustly can cause their followers to exhibit negative behaviors that can be damaging to an individual, the group, and/or the organization. For example, unjust leaders will see decreased motivation among followers or behaviors that harm the people in the organization or even the organization itself. This, of course, will lead to a dysfunctional kingdom or a less-than-ideal workplace.

There are multiple aspects of justice. These include fairness in outcomes, fairness in processes, fairness in interactions, and fairness in information sharing. To be perceived as fair, leaders should consider each of these separate aspects as these four aspects are often viewed as part of an overall gestalt in the minds of the followers regarding how fair (or not) a leader is.

Effective Queens and Kings See Negotiations as an Opportunity to Grow and Receive Positive Outcomes, and They Leverage Negotiation Styles That Best Fit Their Context

Leaders understand the importance of negotiations. Good leaders understand that negotiations represent opportunities to work together, to collaborate, and to learn from others. Negotiations do not need to be confrontational in nature. In fact, sometimes, the most effective leaders have found that negotiating can be very positive and helpful for multiple parties in achieving desired outcomes, or even better-than-desired outcomes.

Negotiating is a process. It includes finding one's relative position as the negotiation gets underway, identifying issues and problems, coming up with ideas for solutions, and then reaching (and following through with) the most optimal solution. Effective leaders understand this process and successfully manage each step of the process.

Different leaders may choose to manage their negotiations in different ways in order to get the most optimal and desirable outcomes possible. Some approaches they can use include tackling multiple issues at the same time, focusing on specific issues, giving in to others' needs, and others. In order to be successful, though, leaders must understand which tactics will work most effectively with the party with whom they are negotiating.

Effective Queens and Kings Seek to Understand Multiple Cultures

Culture is a collective mindset that influences the way that people think, the things that people do, and the values that people care about. As such, it is an important part of a leader's context. Effective leaders understand their culture and leveraging their understanding of the world to connect with others. Though cultures are extremely nuanced, leaders can glean clues about a culture from the artifacts they see, hear, encounter, and experience.

When a leader develops both an awareness of and a sensitivity to multiple cultures, many positive outcomes are likely to occur. For example, mutual trust can be increased, mutual respect among different cultural groups can grow, and people learn to appreciate each other.

Unfortunately, the opposite is also true. Leaders may fail to understand other cultures and/or appreciate cultural differences. When this occurs, business deals and partnerships can be impaired. Moreover, when this happens, people from different cultures will feel less understood and less valued.

It is also important for leaders to understand that cultures are not stagnant. They are dynamic and they change over time. So, leaders need to not only practice cultural sensitivity in the here-and-now, but also keep up with trends that influence how culture changes over time.

Summary

There are many lessons that can be learned from *Game of Thrones*. In the show (and Martin's original writing), there are many examples of both good and bad leaders. From them, multiple best practices can be distilled. This final concluding chapter has attempted to clearly state these practices by briefly summarizing some of the details from earlier in this book. Listed more plainly, these best practices are:

- Effective queens and kings understand their context to inform their leadership styles and activities of making decisions, communicating, and motivating in order to achieve common goals.
- Effective queens and kings know that the traits and behaviors that helped them emerge as leaders will not necessarily make them effective in their roles; they instead learn from challenges, find ways to exert influence that fit their context, and continuously adapt.
- Effective queens and kings leverage multiple bases of power, often alongside servant or transformational leadership approaches, in an ethical manner that is focused on the common good.
- Effective queens and kings communicate in a manner that accurately and truthfully conveys meaning to multiple audiences.
- Effective queens and kings understand the values that they care about and deliberately use them to guide their decisions.
- Effective queens and kings understand how to motivate followers.

- Effective queens and kings know they will not sit on the throne for long if their followers do not trust them, so they actively seek to build and maintain trust.
- Effective queens and kings understand that perceptions of fairness are ultimately linked to their ability to influence.
- Effective queens and kings see negotiations as an opportunity to grow and receive positive outcomes and they leverage negotiating styles that best fit their context.
- Effective queens and kings seek to understand multiple cultures.

We hope you find these recommendations to be helpful as you consider your own leadership style and behaviors. Though every leader's experience is different, having some guidance (even if using examples from the fictional Seven Kingdoms) can help each one to reflect on their own approaches to leadership. And, though each context is different, every leader faces their own set of challenges. We hope this book helps you to face yours effectively, because the night is long and full of darkness ... and winter is coming.

Appendix: List of *Game of Thrones* Characters Mentioned in This Book, with a Brief Description of Each

Character	Brief Description
Arryn, Lysa	Lady Regent of the Vale as the mother of the young Robin Arryn; lives in the Eyrie; older sister to Catelyn Stark
Arryn, Robin	Warden of the East (6 years old at the start of the series); son of Lysa Arryn
Baelish, Petyr "Littlefinger"	Master of Coin under King Robert Baratheon; brothel owner; skilled manipulator
Baratheon, Joffrey	18th King of Westeros; son of Cersei Lannister, fathered by Jamie Lannister but raised as King Robert Baratheon's son; older brother of Myrcella and Tommen Baratheon; poisoned and killed by Olenna Tyrell at his wedding to Margery Tyrell
Baratheon, Myrcella	Daughter of Cersei; sister to Joffrey and Tommen; fathered by Jamie but raised as Robert Baratheon's child; sent off to Dorne
Baratheon, Robert	17th Ruler of Westeros; husband to Cersei Lannister and supposed father to Joffrey, Myrcella, and Tommen; died after being attacked by a wild boar while hunting
Baratheon, Stannis	Younger brother of King Robert Baratheon; believes he is the rightful heir of the Iron Throne after Robert's death
Baratheon, Tommen	19th Ruler of Westeros as King Tommen I; son of Cersei; brother to Joffrey and Myrcella; fathered by Jamie but raised as Robert Baratheon's child; married to Margery Tyrell
Brienne of Tarth	First woman in the Seven Kingdoms to become a knight; swears an oath to Catelyn Stark to protect her and her family
Clegane, Gregor (aka The Mountain)	Reknown fighter famous for his size; older brother of Sandor Clegane; almost killed by Oberyn Martell but revived (in an unnatural state) by Qyburn

(Continued)

Character	Brief Description
Clegane, Sandor (aka The Hound)	Skilled fighter for the Lannisters and personal bodyguard to Joffrey Baratheon but deserts his position; younger brother of Gregor Clegane
Bolton, Ramsay	Legitimized bastard son of Roose Bolton; married to Sansa Stark
Bolton, Roose	Head of House Bolton and Lord of the Dreadfort; father of Ramsay Bolton; appointed as new Warden of the North by King Joffrey
Bronn	Skilled swordsman hired by Tyrion Lannister for protection; works his way up to Lord of Highgarden, Lord Paramount of the Reach, and Master of Coin under King Bran Stark
Frey, Walder	Lord of the Crossing and head of House Frey
Giantsbane, Tormund	Famous fighter among the Free Folk; one of the main leaders under Mance Rayder
Grey Worm	Chosen by his peers as commander of the Unsullied; freed from slavery by, and faithfully serves, Daenerys Targaryen
Greyjoy, Theon (aka Reek)	Son of Balon Greyjoy, King of the Iron Islands; taken as a ward to Ned Stark; referred to ask Reek after enduring torture inflicted by Ramsay Bolton
Jaqen H'ghar	One of the Faceless Men of Braavos, skilled assassin who can change their appearance
Khal Drogo	Famed Dothraki warrior who was never defeated in battle; married to Daenerys Targaryen before his death
Kraznys mo Nakloz	One of the Good Masters of Astapor, slave trader and trainer of the Unsullied soldiers
Lannister, Cersei	20th Ruler of Westeros as Queen Cersei; daughter of Tywin, twin sister to Jamie and older sister of Tyrion
Lanniser, Jamie	Son of Tywin; twin sister to Cersei and older brother of Tyrion; known as "The Kingslayer" after killing the "Mad King," Aerys II Targaryen
Lannister, Kevan	Younger brother of Tywin Lannister; refuses to serve on the small council under Cersei
Lannister, Tyrion	Youngest child of Tywin; brother to Cersei and Jamie; called an imp and a halfman because he is a dwarf; married to Sansa Stark
Lannister, Tywin	Head of House Lannister; father of Cersei, Jamie, and Tyrion

Character	Brief Description
Locke	Roose Bolton's best hunter; best known for dismembering Jamie Lannister's hand
Maester Aemon	Maester at Castle Black; adviser to the Lord Commanders of the Night's Watch; born Aemon Targaryen
Martell, Oberyn	Member of House Martell of Dorne; fights in place of Tyrion Lannister at his trial by combat for Joffrey's death
Melisandre	Often called "the Red Woman," she is a Red Priestess and served as Stannis Baratheon's main adviser in his quest for the Iron Throne
Mero of Braavos	Sellsword from Braavos; one of the captains of the Seven Sons
Missandei	Former slave to Kraznys mo Nakloz; freed by Daenerys Targaryen and loyally serves as her adviser and handmaiden; speaks multiple languages
Mord	Prison guard of the Sky Cells in the Eyrie; cognitively impaired but cruel
Mormont, Jorah	Originally working as a spy for Lord Varys under King Robert Baratheon, he becomes adviser and protector to Daenerys Targaryen
Naharis, Daario	Initially a lieutenant from the Second Sons, he becomes an adviser and lover to Daenerys Targaryen
no one	One of the Faceless Men of Braavos; bears the face of Jaqen H'ghar
Prendahl na Ghezen	One of the captains of the Second Sons of Braavos
Qyburn	Former maester with questionable ethics; serves as Hand of the Queen to Cersei Lannister
Rayder, Mance	Leader of the Free Folk; named King-Beyond-the-Wall by the Free Folk
Seaworth, Davros	Knight who served Stannis Baratheon; after Stannis's death, he persuades Melisandre to bring Jon Snow back from the dead; serves on the small council for King Bran
Shae	Former prostitute; mistress to Tyrion Lannister, although she ultimately betrays him
Snow, Jon	998th Lord Commander of the Night's Watch; bastard son of Ned Stark, although it is revealed that he is actually a Targaryen
Stark, Arya	Youngest daughter of Ned and Catelyn Stark; sister to Robb, Sansa, and Bran

(Continued)

Character	Brief Description
Stark, Brandon (Bran)	Second son of Ned and Catelyn Stark; crowned as King Bran I the Broken at the end of the series
Stark, Catelyn	Lady of Winterfell and wife to Ned Stark; mother of Robb, Sansa, Arya, and Bran (and Rickon) Stark
Stark, Eddard "Ned"	Lord of Winterfell and Warden of the North; Hand of the King to Robert Baratheon before Robert's death; beheaded by King Joffrey Baratheon
Stark, Robb	Firstborn son of Ned Stark; named King in the North after his father's death, before his own death at the hands of Roose Bolton
Stark, Sansa	Oldest daughter of Ned and Catelyn Stark; married to Tyrion Lannister and Ramsay Bolton; crowned as Queen of the North at the of the series
Targaryen, Aerys II (The "Mad King")	Former King of Westeros; slain by Jamie Lannister and replaced by Robert Baratheon; father to Viserys and Daenerys Targaryen
Targaryen, Daenerys	Daughter of Aerys II and younger sister of Viserys; Mother of Dragons; believes she is the rightful heir to the Iron Throne after her father's death; frees the Unsullied and Slaver's Bay
Targaryen, Viserys	Son of Aerys II and older brother of Daenerys; marries off his sister to the Dothraki in exchange for soldiers in his quest for the Iron Throne
Tarly, Samwell (Sam)	Disinherited by his father and sent to join the Night's Watch as his only option to live; overweight with poor eyesight, he prefers books and knowledge over swords and combat; best friend to Jon Snow
Tyrell, Loras	Heir to Highgarden; grandson of Olenna Tyrell and younger brother to Margaery Tyrell; one of the most skilled knights in Westeros
Tyrell, Margery	Queen of Westeros when she was married to Joffrey Baratheon and later to Tommen Baratheon; older sister of Loras Tyrell and granddaughter to Olenna Tyrell
Tyrell, Olenna (Lady Olenna)	Matriarch of House Tyrell; responsible for Joffrey Baratheon's murder
Varys (Lord Varys)	Astute manipulator with numerous informants; Master of Whispers under multiple kings of Westeros; claims loyalty to the realm rather than any one king or house
Ygritte	A woman of the Free Folk (a Wildling) and Jon Snow's lover

References

Adair, W. L., & Brett, J. M. (2005). The negotiation dance: Time, culture, and behavioral sequences in negotiation. *Organization Science, 16*(1), 33–51.

Ambrose, M. L., & Schminke, M. (2009). The role of overall justice judgments in organizational justice research: A test of mediation. *Journal of Applied Psychology, 94*(2), 491–500.

Ang, S., Van Dyne, L., Koh, C., Ng, K. Y., Templer, K. J., Tay, C., & Chandrasekar, N. A. (2007). Cultural intelligence: Its measurement and effects on cultural judgment and decision making, cultural adaptation and task performance. *Management and Organization Review, 3*(3), 335–371.

Antonakis, J., Fenley, M., & Liechti, S. (2011). Can charisma be taught? Tests of two interventions. *Academy of Management Learning & Education, 10*(3), 374–396.

Antonakis, J., & House, R. J. (2002). The full-range leadership theory: The way forward. In B. Avolio & F. Yammarino (Eds.), *Transformational and charismatic leadership: The road ahead* (pp. 3–34). JAI.

Avolio, B. J., Waldman, D. A., & Yammarino, F. J. (1991). Leading in the 1990s: The Four I's of transformational leadership. *Journal of European Industrial Training, 15*(4), 9–16.

Ayres, I. (1991). Fair driving: Gender and race discrimination in retail car negotiations. *Harvard Law Review, 104*(4), 817–872.

Bargh, J. A., & Williams, E. L. (2006). The automaticity of social life. *Current Directions in Psychological Science, 15*(1), 1–4.

Barton, S. L., Duchon, D., & Dunegan, K. J. (1989). An empirical test of Staw and Ross's prescriptions for the management of escalation of commitment behavior in organizations. *Decision Sciences, 20*, 532–544.

Baum, J. R., & Locke, E. A. (2004). The relationship of entrepreneurial traits, skill, and motivation to subsequent venture growth. *Journal of Applied Psychology, 89*(4), 587–598.

Beersma, B., & De Dreu, C. K. (2002). Integrative and distributive negotiation in small groups: Effects of task structure, decision rule, and social motive. *Organizational Behavior and Human Decision Processes, 87*(2), 227–252.

Bews, N. F., & Rossouw, G. J. (2002). A role for business ethics in facilitating trustworthiness. *Journal of Business Ethics, 39*(4), 377–390.

Bies, R. J., & Moag, J. S. (1986). Processual justice: Communicating criteria of fairness. In R. J. Lewicki, B. H. Sheppard, & M. H. Bazerman (Eds.), *Research on negotiation in organizations*. JAI Press.

Blanchard, K. H., & Hersey, P. (1996). Great ideas revisited. *Training & Development, 50*(1), 42–48.

Blau, P. M. (1964). Justice in social exchange. *Sociological Inquiry, 34*(2), 193–206.

Brockner, J., Siegel, P. A., Daly, J. P., Tyler, T., & Martin, C. (1997). When trust matters: The moderating effect of outcome favorability. *Administrative Science Quarterly, 42*(3), 558–583.

Broeder, P. (2021). Informed communication in high context and low context cultures. *Journal of Education, Innovation, and Communication, 3*(1), 13–24.

Byrne, A., Crossan, M., & Seijts, G. (2018). The development of leader character through crucible moments. *Journal of Management Education, 42*(2), 265–293.

Child, J. (1972). Organizational structure, environment, and performance: The role of strategic choice. *Sociology, 6,* 1–22.

Collins, J. (2009). *Good to Great—(Why some companies make the leap and others don't).* HarperCollins.

Collins, J. M., & Griffin R.W. (1998). In R. W. Griffin, A. O'Leary-Kelly, & J. M. Collins (Eds.), *Dysfunctional behavior in organizations: Violent and deviant behavior.* JAI Press.

Colquitt, J. A. (2001). On the dimensionality of organizational justice: A construct validation of a measure. *Journal of Applied Psychology, 86*(3), 386–400.

Colquitt, J. A., Conlon, D. E., Wesson, M. J., Porter, C. O., & Ng, K. Y. (2001). Justice at the millennium: A meta-analytic review of 25 years of organizational justice research. *Journal of Applied Psychology, 86*(3), 425–445.

Colquitt, J. A., & Rodell, J. B. (2011). Justice, trust, and trustworthiness: A longitudinal analysis integrating three theoretical perspectives. *Academy of Management Journal, 54*(6), 1183–1206.

Congdon, K. G. (1984). A folkloric approach to studying folk art: Benefits for cultural awareness. *Journal of Cultural Research in Art Education, 2*(1), 5–13.

Conger, J. A., Kanungo, R. N., & Menon, S. T. (2000). Charismatic leadership and follower effects. *Journal of Organizational Behavior: The International Journal of Industrial, Occupational and Organizational Psychology and Behavior, 21*(7), 747–767.

Cotter, M. J., & Henley, J. A. (2008). First-offer disadvantage in zero-sum game negotiation outcomes. *Journal of Business-to-Business Marketing, 15*(1), 25–44.

D'Cruz, P., Noronha, E., & Lutgen-Sandvik, P. (2018). Power, subjectivity and context in workplace bullying, emotional abuse and harassment: Insights from postpositivism. *Qualitative Research in Organizations and Management, 13*(1), 2–9. https://doi.org/10.1108/QROM-12-2017-1587

Dansereau, F., Graen, G., & Haga, W. J. (1975). A vertical dyad linkage approach to leadership within formal organizations: A longitudinal investigation of the role making process. *Organizational Behavior and Human Decision Processes, 13*(1), 46–78.

Daft, R. L. (2014). *The Leadership Experience.* Cengage Learning.

de Wet C., & Jacobs L. (2021). Workplace bullying, emotional abuse and harassment in schools. In P. D'Cruz, E. Noronha, L. Keashly, & S. Tye-Williams (Eds.), *Special topics and particular occupations, professions and sectors. Handbooks of workplace bullying, emotional abuse and harassment* (Vol 4). Springer. https://doi.org/10.1007/978-981-10-5308-5_11

Dean, J. S., Gumerman, G. J., Epstein, J. M., Axtell, R. L., Swedlund, A. C., Parker, M. T., & McCarroll, S. (2000). Understanding Anasazi culture change through agent-based modeling. In T. Kohler & G. Gumerman (Eds.), *Dynamics in human and primate societies: Agent-based modeling of social and spatial processes* (pp. 179–205). Oxford University Press.

DeShon, R. P., Kozlowski, S. W., Schmidt, A. M., Milner, K. R., & Wiechmann, D. (2004). A multiple-goal, multilevel model of feedback effects on the regulation of individual and team performance. *Journal of Applied Psychology, 89*(6), 1035–1056.

Deutsch, M. (1973). *The resolution of conflict: Constructive and destructive processes.* Yale University Press.

Drach-Zahavy, A., & Erez, M. (2002). Challenge versus threat effects on the goal–performance relationship. *Organizational Behavior and Human Decision Processes, 88*(2), 667–682.

Earley, P. C., & Ang, S. (2003). *Cultural intelligence: Individual interactions across cultures.* Stanford University Press.

Eisenhardt, K. M. (1989). Agency theory: An assessment and review. *Academy of Management Review, 14*(1), 57–74.

Ensari, N., Riggio, R. E., Christian, J., & Carslaw, G. (2011). Who emerges as a leader? Meta-analyses of individual differences as predictors of leadership emergence. *Personality and Individual Differences, 51*(4), 532–536.

Fairhurst, G. T. (2010). *The power of framing: Creating the language of leadership*. Jossey-Bass.

Fairhurst, G. T., & Connaughton, S. L. (2014). Leadership: A communicative perspective. *Leadership, 10*(1), 7–35.

Fiol, C. M., Harris, D., & House, R. (1999). Charismatic leadership: Strategies for effecting social change. *The Leadership Quarterly, 10*(3), 449–482.

Fleishman, E. A., & Peters, D. R. (1962). Interpersonal values, leadership attitudes and managerial success. *Personnel Psychology, 15*(2), 127–143.

Folger, R. (1977). Distributive and procedural justice: Combined impact of voice and improvement on experienced inequity. *Journal of Personality and Social Psychology, 35*(2), 108–119.

Fox, M. A. (2018). Drive-in theatres, technology, and cultural change. *Economics, Management, and Financial Markets, 13*(2), 24–39.

Fox, S., Spector, P. E., & Miles, D. (2001). Counterproductive work behavior (CWB) in response to job stressors and organizational justice: Some mediator and moderator tests for autonomy and emotions. *Journal of Vocational Behavior, 59*(3), 291–309.

French, J. R. P., Jr, & Raven, B. (1959). The bases of social power. In D. Cartwright (Ed.), *Studies in social power* (pp. 150–167). Institute for Social Research.

Froman, L. A., Jr, & Cohen, M. D. (1970). Compromise and logroll: Comparing the efficiency of two bargaining processes. *Behavioral Science, 15*(2), 180–183.

Fryer, M. (2012). Facilitative leadership: Drawing on Jürgen Habermas' model of ideal speech to propose a less impositional way to lead. *Organization, 19*(1), 25–43.

Galbraith, J., & Cummings, L. L. (1967). An empirical investigation of the motivational determinants of task performance: Interactive effects between instrumentality—valence and motivation—ability. *Organizational Behavior and Human Performance, 2*(3), 237–257.

Galinsky, A. D., & Mussweiler, T. (2001). First offers as anchors: The role of perspective taking and negotiator focus. *Journal of Personality and Social Psychology, 81*(4), 657–669.

Game of Thrones Awards and Nominations. (n.d.). Emmys. Retrieved September 14, 2022, from https://www.emmys.com/shows/game-thrones

Gebert, D., Boerner, S., & Kearney, E. (2010). Fostering team innovation: Why is it important to combine opposing action strategies? *Organization Science, 21*(3), 593–608.

Geiger, I. (2017). A model of negotiation issue-based tactics in business-to-business sales negotiations. *Industrial Marketing Management, 64*, 91–106.

Gillespie, N. A., & Mann, L. (2004). Transformational leadership and shared values: The building blocks of trust. *Journal of Managerial Psychology, 19*(6), 588–607.

Goldsmith, M. (2010). *What got you here won't get you there: How successful people become even more successful*. Profile Books.

Govindarajan, V., & Gupta, A. K. (2001). Building an effective global business team. *MIT Sloan Management Review, 42*(4), 63–71.

Graen, G., & Uhl-Bien, M. (1995). Relation-based approach to leadership: Development of leader–member exchange (LMX) theory of leadership over 25 years: Applying a multi-level multi-domain perspective. *Leadership Quarterly, 6*(2), 219–247.

Greenberg, J. (2001). Setting the justice agenda: Seven unanswered questions about "what, why, and how." *Journal of Vocational Behavior, 58*(2), 210–219.

Greenberg, J., & Tyler, T. R. (1987). Why procedural justice in organizations? *Social Justice Research, 1*(2), 127–142.

Greenleaf, R. K. (1977). *Servant leadership: A journey into the nature of legitimate power and greatness*. Paulist Press.

Hart, A., Toma, M., Issa, F., & Ciottone, G. R. (2019). Absence of cultural awareness training in international non-governmental organizations. *Prehospital and Disaster Medicine, 34*(5), 486–488.

Harton, H. C., & Bourgeois, M. J. (2003). Cultural elements emerge from dynamic social impact. In M. Schaller & C. S. Crandall (Eds.), *The psychological foundations of culture* (pp. 50–85). Erlbaum Associates.

Hoffman, B. J., Blair, C. A., Meriac, J. P., & Woehr, D. J. (2007). Expanding the criterion domain? A quantitative review of the OCB literature. *Journal of Applied Psychology, 92*(2), 555.

Hoffman, D. A., & Triantafillou, K. (2014). Cultural and diversity issues in mediation and negotiation. In R. Parekh (Ed.), *The Massachusetts general hospital textbook on diversity and cultural sensitivity in mental health* (pp. 229–251). Humana Press.

Hofstede, G. (2011). Dimensionalizing cultures: The Hofstede Model in context. *Online Readings in Psychology and Culture, Unit 2*. http://scholarworks.gvsu.edu/orpc/vol2/iss1/8

Hogan, J., & Hogan, R. (1989). How to measure employee reliability. *Journal of Applied Psychology, 74*(2), 273–279.

Hogg, M. A., Terry, D. J., & White, K. M. (1995). A tale of two theories: A critical comparison of identity theory with social identity theory. *Social Psychology Quarterly, 58*(4), 255–269.

Holtz, B. C., & Harold, C. M. (2013). Interpersonal justice and deviance: The moderating effects of interpersonal justice values and justice orientation. *Journal of Management, 39*(2), 339–365.

Hüffmeier, J., Freund, P. A., Zerres, A., Backhaus, K., & Hertel, G. (2014). Being tough or being nice? A meta-analysis on the impact of hard- and softline strategies in distributive negotiations. *Journal of Management, 40*(3), 866–892.

IMDb TV Series (Sorted by Number of Votes Descending). (n.d.). IMDb. Retrieved September 14, 2022, from https://www.imdb.com/search/title/?sort=num_votes, desc&title_type=tv_series

Johnson, J. J., & Cullen, J. B. (2002). Trust in cross-cultural relationships. In M. J. Gannon and K. L. Newman (Eds.), *Blackwell handbook of cross-cultural management* (pp. 335–360). Blackwell.

Judge, T. A., Piccolo, R. F., & Ilies, R. (2004). The forgotten ones? The validity of consideration and initiating structure in leadership research. *Journal of Applied Psychology, 89*(1), 36–51.

Judge, T. A., Piccolo, R. F., & Kosalka, T. (2009). The bright and dark sides of leader traits: A review and theoretical extension of the leader trait paradigm. *The Leadership Quarterly, 20*(6), 855–875.

Kahneman, D., & A. Tversky. (1979). Prospect theory: An analysis of decision under risk. *Econometrica, 47*, 263–291.

Kanwal, I., Lodhi, R. N., & Kashif, M. (2019). Leadership styles and workplace ostracism among frontline employees. *Management Research Review, 42*(8), 991–1013.

Kohlberg, L. (1969). Stage and sequence: The cognitive developmental approach to socialization. In D. A. Goslin (Ed.), *Handbook of socialization theory and research* (pp. 347–480). Rand McNally.

Kreiner, G. E., & Ashforth, B. E. (2004). Evidence toward an expanded model of organizational identification. *Journal of Organizational Behavior: The International Journal of Industrial, Occupational and Organizational Psychology and Behavior, 25*(1), 1–27.

Krone, K. J., Jablin, F. M., & Putnam, L. L. (1987). *Communication theory and organizational communication: Multiple perspectives*. In F. M. Jablin, L. L. Putnam, K. H. Roberts, & L. W. Porter (Eds.), *Handbook of organizational communication*. Sage.

Latham, G. P., & Pinder, C. C. (2005). Work motivation theory and research at the dawn of the twenty-first century. *Annual Review of Psychology, 56*(1), 485–516.

Leventhal, G. S. (1980). What should be done with equity theory? New approaches to the study of fairness in social relationships. In K. Gergen, M. Greenberg, & R. Willis (Eds.), *Social exchanges: Advances in theory and research* (pp. 27–55). New York: Plenum.

Lewicki, R. J., Barry, B., & Saunders, D. (2010). *Negotiation* (6th edition). Burr Ridge, IL: McGraw-Hill Irwin.

Lewis, J. D., & Weigert, A. (1985). Trust as a social reality. *Social Forces, 63*, 967–985.

Liden, R., & Graen, G. (1980). Generalizability of the vertical dyad linkage model of leadership. *Academy of Management Journal, 23*(2), 1090–1109.

Lind, E. A., Kanfer, R., & Earley, P. C. (1990). Voice, control, and procedural justice: Instrumental and noninstrumental concerns in fairness judgments. *Journal of Personality and Social Psychology, 59*(5), 952–959.

Lind, E. A., & Tyler, T. R. (1988). *The social psychology of procedural justice.* Springer Science & Business Media.

Locke, E. A., & Latham, G. P. (1990). *A theory of goal setting & task performance.* Prentice-Hall, Inc.

Locke, E. A., & Latham, G. P. (2002). Building a practically useful theory of goal setting and task motivation: A 35-year odyssey. *American Psychologist, 57*(9), 705–717.

Locke, E. A., & Latham, G. P. (2006). New directions in goal-setting theory. *Current Directions in Psychological Science, 15*(5), 265–268.

Mainiero, L. (2020). Workplace romance versus sexual harassment: A call to action regarding sexual hubris and sexploitation in the #MeToo era. *Gender in Management, 35*(4), 329–347. https://doi.org/10.1108/GM-11-2019-0198

Mannix, E. A., Thompson, L. L., & Bazerman, M. H. (1989). Negotiation in small groups. *Journal of Applied Psychology, 74*(3), 508–517.

Martinko, M. J., Gundlach, M. J., & Douglas, S. C. (2002). Toward an integrative theory of counterproductive workplace behavior: A causal reasoning perspective. *International Journal of Selection and Assessment, 10*(1–2), 36–50.

Masterson, S. S. (2001). A trickle-down model of organizational justice: Relating employees' and customers' perceptions of and reactions to fairness. *Journal of Applied Psychology, 86*(4), 594–604.

Mayer, R. C., Davis, J. H., & Schoorman, F. D. (1995). An integrative model of organizational trust. *Academy of Management Review, 20*(3), 709–734.

McAllister, D. J. (1995). Affect- and cognition-based trust as foundations for interpersonal cooperation in organizations. *Academy of Management Journal, 38*(1), 24–59.

McAuley, E., Wraith, S., & Duncan, T. E. (1991). Self-efficacy, perceptions of success, and intrinsic motivation for exercise 1. *Journal of Applied Social Psychology, 21*(2), 139–155.

McKnight, D. H., Cummings, L. L., & Chervany, N. L. (1998). Initial trust formation in new organizational relationships. *Academy of Management Review, 23*(3), 473–490.

Merriam-Webster. (n.d.). *Crucible.* https://www.merriam-webster.com/dictionary/crucible.

Merriam-Webster. (n.d.). *Influence.* https://www.merriam-webster.com/dictionary/influence

O'Keefe, B. J., & McCornack, S. A. (1987). Message design logic and message goal structure: Effects on perceptions of message quality in regulative communication situations. *Human Communication Research, 14*(1), 68–92.

Organ, D. W. (1988). *Organizational citizenship behavior: The good solider syndrome.* Lexington Books.

Organ, D. W. (1990). The motivational basis of organizational citizenship behavior. In B. M. Staw & L. L. Cummings (Eds.), *Research in organizational behavior* (Vol. 12, pp. 43–72). JAI Press.

Patient, D. L., & Skarlicki, D. P. (2010). Increasing interpersonal and informational justice when communicating negative news: The role of the manager's empathic concern and moral development. *Journal of Management, 36*(2), 555–578.

Patton, C., & Balakrishnan, P. V. (2010). The impact of expectation of future negotiation interaction on bargaining processes and outcomes. *Journal of Business Research*, *63*(8), 809–816.

Pennings, J. M., & Woiceshyn, J. (1987). *A typology of organizational control and its metaphors: Research in the sociology of organizations*. JAI Press.

Podsakoff, P. M., Ahearne, M., & MacKenzie, S. B. (1997). Organizational citizenship behavior and the quantity and quality of work group performance. *Journal of Applied Psychology*, *82*, 262–270.

Pruitt, D. G. (1971). Indirect communication and the search for agreement in negotiation. *Journal of Applied Social Psychology*, *1*(3), 205–239.

Pyszczynski, T. A., & Greenberg, J. (1981). Role of disconfirmed expectancies in the instigation of attributional processing. *Journal of Personality and Social Psychology*, *40*(1), 31–38.

Rest, J. (1986). *Manual for the defining issues test*. Center for the Study of Ethical Development.

Robert, L. P., Denis, A. R., & Hung, Y. T. C. (2009). Individual swift trust and knowledge-based trust in face-to-face and virtual team members. *Journal of Management Information Systems*, *26*(2), 241–279.

Rotten Tomatoes Fall. (2017). 40 Best TV Shows of the Past 20 Years. (n.d.). Rotten Tomatoes. Retrieved September 14, 2022, from https://editorial.rottentomatoes.com/guide/best-tv-shows-of-the-past-20-years-2017-survey/

Seijts, G. H., & Latham, G. P. (2000). The effects of goal setting and group size on performance in a social dilemma. *Canadian Journal of Behavioural Science/Revue Canadienne des Sciences du Comportement*, *32*(2), 104–116.

Seijts, G. H., & Latham, G. P. (2001). The effect of distal learning, outcome, and proximal goals on a moderately complex task. *Journal of Organizational Behavior: The International Journal of Industrial, Occupational and Organizational Psychology and Behavior*, *22*(3), 291–307.

Senge, P. M. (2006). *The fifth discipline: The art and practice of the learning organization*. Currency.

Shamir, B., & Howell, J. M. (1999). Organizational and contextual influences on the emergence and effectiveness of charismatic leadership. *The Leadership Quarterly*, *10*, 257–283.

Shannon, C. E., & Weaver, W. (1964). *The mathematical theory of communication*. University of Illinois Press.

Shell, G. R. (2006). *Bargaining for advantage: Negotiation strategies for reasonable people*. Penguin Books.

Shennan, S. (2000). Population, culture history, and the dynamics of culture change. *Current Anthropology*, *41*(5), 811–835.

Short, J. A. (1974). Effects of medium of communication on experimental negotiation. *Human Relations*, *27*(3), 225–234.

Stack, S. (1978). The effect of direct government involvement in the economy on the degree of income inequality: A cross-national study. *American Sociological Review*, *43*(6), 880–888.

Stajkovic, A. D., Locke, E. A., & Blair, E. S. (2006). A first examination of the relationships between primed subconscious goals, assigned conscious goals, and task performance. *Journal of Applied Psychology*, *91*(5), 1172–1180.

Statista. (2021, January 13). *Game of Thrones fans in the U.S. 2019*. Retrieved September 14, 2022, from https://www.statista.com/statistics/991024/game-of-thrones-fans-in-the-us/

Staw, B. M. (1976). Knee-deep in the big muddy: A study of escalating commitment to choosing a course of action. *Organizational Behavior and Human Performance, 16,* 27–44.

Staw, B. M. (1981). The escalation of commitment to a course of action. *Academy of Management Review, 6,* 577–587.

Staw, B. M., & Ross, J. (1978). Commitment to a policy decision: A multi-theoretical perspective. *Administrative Science Quarterly, 23,* 40–64.

Staw, B. M., & Ross, J. (1987). Knowing when to pull the plug. *Harvard Business Review, 65,* 68–74.

Stone, A. G., Russell, R. F., & Patterson, K. (2004). Transformational versus servant leadership: A difference in leader focus. *Leadership & Organization Development Journal, 25*(4), 349–361.

Tajfel, H., & Turner, J. C. (1979). An integrative theory of inter-group conflict. In W. G. Austin & S. Worchel (Eds.), *The social psychology of inter-group relations* (pp. 33–47). Brooks/Cole.

Tajfel, H., & Turner, J. C. (2004). The social identity theory of intergroup behavior. In *Political psychology* (pp. 276–293). Psychology Press.

The Hollywood Reporter. https://www.hollywoodreporter.com/tv/tv-news/game-thrones-series-finale-sets-all-time-hbo-ratings-record-1212269/

Thompson, L. L., Mannix, E. A., & Bazerman, M. H. (1988). Group negotiation: Effects of decision rule, agenda, and aspiration. *Journal of Personality and Social Psychology, 54*(1), 86–95.

Thompson, L. L., Wang, J., & Gunia, B. C. (2010). Negotiation. *Annual Review of Psychology, 61,* 491–515.

Trevino, L. K., & Nelson, K. A. (2007). *Managing business ethics: Straight talk about how to do it right* (4th ed.). John Wiley and Sons, In.

Urick, M. J. (2021). *Leadership in middle-earth: Theories and applications for organizations.* Emerald Group Publishing.

Urick, M. J., & Racculia, N. (2017). ethical decision making in Game of Thrones: Applying leadership from Westeros to business. *Journal of Leadership and Management, 1*(9–10), 9–16.

van Dierendonck, D. (2011). Servant leadership: A review and synthesis. *Journal of Management, 37*(4), 1228–1261.

Vroom, V. H. (1964). *Work and motivation.* Wiley.

Vroom, V. H., & Jago, A. G. (2007). The role of the situation in leadership. *American Psychologist, 62*(1), 17–24.

Vroom, V. H., & Yetton, P. W. (1973). *Leadership and decision-making.* University of Pittsburgh Press.

Waldman, D. A., Bass, B. M., & Yammarino, F. J. (1990). Adding to contingent-reward behavior: The augmenting effect of charismatic leadership. *Group & Organization Studies, 15*(4), 381–394.

Webb, W. M., Worchel, S., & Brown, E. H. (1986). The influence of control on self-attributions. *Social Psychology Quarterly, 49*(3), 260–267.

Weick, K. E. (1995). *Sensemaking in organizations* (Vol. 3). Sage.

Weischer, A. E., Weibler, J., & Petersen, M. (2013). To thine own self be true: The effects of enactment and life storytelling on perceived leader authenticity. *The Leadership Quarterly, 24*(4), 477–495.

Wilkens, S. (2011). *Beyond bumper sticker ethics: An introduction to theories of right and wrong,* 2nd edition. InterVarsity Press.

Wong, P. T., & Weiner, B. (1981). When people ask "why" questions, and the heuristics of attributional search. *Journal of Personality and Social Psychology, 40*(4), 650–663.

Index